THE Ornate Lock

The Psychology of Malyalam Movies

Dr. Robin K Mathew

Writer's Pocket

First published by Writer's Pocket in 2026

email: editor@writerspocket.com

Cover Design by Dr Robin K Mathew

ISBN-13: 978-93-7248-622-3

www.writerspocket.com

"Dedicated to the souls who poured their life's blood and every heartbeat into the magic of the silver screen. You are the invisible pulse behind every story ever told."

CONTENTS

Chapter 1

Manichitrathazhu

Director: Fazil
Music: M.G. Radhakrishnan
Cast: Shobhana, Mohanlal, Suresh Gopi, Vinaya Prasad, Nedumudi Venu, Thilakan, Innocent, KPAC Lalitha, Sudheesh

When released in 1993, Manichitrathazhu became both a big box-office success and a critic favourite. Even now, many years later, it is still a movie with a cult following. It is hard to find a Malayali who does not remember Nagavalli or who does not react when they hear the line, "Vidamaate?" ("You won't let me go?!"). The film mixes suspense, horror, and psychological drama, and it went on to become a landmark for Indian cinema.

The Plot

Unnithan (Innocent) is the self-declared caretaker of Madampally tharavadu, an old ancestral house. He is getting the place ready because a new heir is coming to live there. The house has been empty for some time, and the local villagers believe it is haunted. After the previous owner died, it was locked up.

Now Nakulan, the current heir, has decided he will move in. But something inside the house scares Unnithan so badly that he runs away in a panic and forgets to take the keys. Later that night, when he remembers, he goes back with Dasappan (Ganesh Kumar) to fetch them. Once again, strange things happen, and both of them rush out in fear.

We learn that, earlier, a spirit was supposedly trapped inside one of the rooms through an exorcism, and after that, the house was sealed.

Thampi (Nedumudi Venu) is the head of the family now. Nakulan (Suresh Gopi) and his wife Ganga (Shobhana) had reached there. Nakulan introduces Ganga to everyone, including Sreedevi (Vinaya Prasad), Thampi's eldest daughter. Ganga senses some hidden tension, even though Sreedevi behaves kindly and politely. Nakulan explains that he is setting up a factory nearby and wants to stay at Madampally while he supervises the work. Thampi is alarmed. He says that, although Nakulan's mother also has a claim to the house, the place is not suitable for anyone to live in. Many unnatural deaths have taken place there, and women who married into the family have suffered badly. He assumes Nakulan must have heard these stories as a child. Nakulan laughs them off and says he does not believe in such tales.

So Nakulan and Ganga move into Madampally.

Haunted Rooms

Slowly, the couple settles into the house. Ganga, who is quiet and thoughtful, falls in love with the calm beauty of the village and the surrounding countryside. She becomes close to Nakulan's cousins Alli and is thrilled to discover that one of her favourite writers is engaged to Alli. The writer lives near their outhouse.

Thampi later tells Ganga that some rooms must remain closed. He explains that the spirits of two youngsters who died unnatural deaths are believed to be shut inside those rooms. Once a year, on Durgashtami, the rooms are opened for rituals meant to keep the spirits under control. He warns her clearly not to try to enter them. Ganga feels uneasy but also curious.

Bhasura Nakulan's aunt later gives Ganga a more detailed story. Many generations ago, an ancestor brought home a dancer from Tamil Nadu as his mistress and kept her in that very suite of rooms. Her name was Nagavalli. She was in love with a young man named Ramanathan, who followed her to Kerala and stayed in the outhouse. When the lord of the house discovered their relationship, he killed Nagavalli. According to the legend, eight days after her death, on Durgashtami, she returned as a yakshi to take revenge. Powerful tantric scholars then performed a ritual that lasted sixty-one days to confine her spirit to that room. The nobleman later committed suicide, and people say his soul also remains trapped in that part of the house.

Ganga is scared but also excited by this story.

She begins to clean out the dusty, cobweb-filled chambers. While she is doing this, Sreedevi rushes in, having heard that a new key has been made for the forbidden room. She tries to stop Ganga from opening the rooms and begs her not to go inside. Ganga laughs off the fears and asks how anything bad can come from a room in their own house. She asks Sreedevi if she really believes all these old tales. Sreedevi herself is confused. She knows that the locksmith who made the new key suddenly developed painful sores, and the boy who gave him the original key came down with a high fever. Worried, Sreedevi decides to shift to the main houseF. Ganga is left wondering what to believe.

Thampi is very anxious now. He feels his niece and nephew are too "modern" and stubborn to accept the idea of danger from spirits. He decides he will not rest until the priests return, repeat the rituals, and reseal the rooms. While Thampi focuses on religious ceremonies, Ganga keeps cleaning and arranging things inside the locked suite.

Voices, Anklets, and Fear

One day, after the rituals are over, Thampi, Dasappan, and the priest go to Madampally to place a purified sacred pot inside the room and close it properly. As they approach, they hear someone speaking Tamil from inside. Shaken, Thampi asks who is there. The reply comes: "Nagavalli." When they hear anklets from within and the door moves, they lose courage and run for their lives. The sacred pot falls and breaks behind them as they flee.

That night, Alli's fiancé, the writer staying in the outhouse, hears anklets and glimpses a woman in white. Moments later, a scream echoes from the main house.

The terrified maid tells Nakulan, Ganga, and Sreedevi that she saw a woman with loose hair at the window. Nakulan dismisses it as superstition and goes back to sleep, but a clay water pot beside him suddenly shatters. Soon, all the kitchen china is found smashed.

The next day, the family gathers at Madampally. Uncles and relatives urge Nakulan to leave, calling the house cursed. Before Nakulan can respond, Ganga suddenly screams—her reaction convinces him the problem is grave. He quietly asks Thampi if any relative has a history of mental illness.

Thampi explodes, blaming Nakulan and his "modern" wife Ganga for the troubles, while defending Sreedevi. He reminds everyone that he, Dasappan, and the tantric all saw the dancer in the sealed south wing. Nakulan insists there must be a rational explanation; the argument ends in anger.

Unnithan proposes a different theory: Sreedevi might be possessed by Nagavalli's spirit, which would explain both the sightings and Nakulan's skepticism. Sreedevi's parents are horrified, but her increasingly strange behaviour soon makes them fear Unnithan is right.

Meanwhile, Nakulan urgently tries to reach his psychiatrist friend. At the same time, Ganga learns the backstory: Sreedevi (Nakulan's first cousin) has chovva dosham (maanglik dosha), yet her horoscope perfectly matched Nakulan's. Nakulan's mother rejected the alliance, soNakulan married Ganga. Thampi hastily married Sreedevi to another man without disclosing the dosham. When the groom discovered it later, he sent Sreedevi back home.

Dr. Sunny Joseph (Mohanlal) arrives as the psychiatrist. His playful, almost madcap behavior shocks the family, but he quietly begins observing everyone and investigating the hauntings. Soon he personally witnesses the eerie events.

A sudden attack on Alli escalates the terror. Nakulan blames Sreedevi; Sunny refuses to conclude yet. A shaken Thampi invites the renowned tantric Brahmaduttan Nampoothiri (Thilakan).

Sunny meets an offended Sreedevi, whose anger grows at his childish antics. That night he hears anklets, a Tamil song, and dancing behind locked doors.

Next day, Ganga shows Sunny Nagavalli's haunted room, her portraits, jewellery, and the outhouse where Ramanathan once stayed. Sunny, secretly forming a plan, asks Nakulan to bring Sreedevi to the temple; there Sunny and Ganga argue.

That night Sunny waits again. When the music stops, a woman's voice in pure Tamil speaks from inside the sealed room. Sunny replies in Tamil, impersonating Sankaran Thampi (Nagavalli's killer). The voice, claiming to be Nagavalli, curses him and vows to kill him on Durgashtami. Sunny, still in character, tells her to return on that day. When the voice ceases, he opens the door—room empty.

Sunny confides in Chandu who is Sreedevi's younger brother. Meanwhile, Brahmaduttan reads the family horoscopes and gravely warns Thampi to be extremely careful, heightening everyone's fear. Sunny realizes that in this atmosphere even murder is possible.

On the night before Durgashtami, during the Kathakali performance at the temple, Alli's fiancé — the writer staying in the outhouse — appears to try to molest Ganga, throwing the whole household into even greater turmoil. What is really happening at Madampally tharavadu? Is Nagavalli's spirit truly seeking revenge? Is Sreedevi possessed? Why is Ganga now being targeted? And who can stop the impending disaster?

Themes, Style, and Performances

Manichitrathazhu received the National Award for Best Popular Film. Fazil is credited as the director, with Sibi Malayil, Priyadarshan, and Siddique-Lal working as second-unit directors. The movie is built like a jigsaw puzzle. At any moment, the audience sees only a part of the full picture. Past and present, myth and reality, truth and lies all move side by side, so viewers keep guessing until the final reveal.

Madhu Muttam, who wrote the story, screenplay, and dialogues, mixes folklore with a thriller about ghosts, possession, and multiple personality disorder. In doing so, he creates Ganga/Nagavalli as a layered and fascinating character.

Like many classic Malayalam films, Manichitrathazhu does not hurry. Instead of rushing through the plot, it takes time to show the village, the old house, and the people who belong there. The first half may feel slow, but it quietly introduces every important character and detail. Later, even a small incident from earlier becomes meaningful, so it rewards viewers who pay attention.

As the events unfold, the audience is pulled into the mystery. Almost every scene raises a question: Are we seeing mental illness, or is this a genuine case of possession?

Malayalam cinema has shown mental illness many times, but it is rare to see it explained in such a way that both the symptoms and the underlying causes are explored. At the same time, the film never completely takes away the feeling that something supernatural might still be happening. You are left wondering: What if the doctor is wrong? What if a spirit is really involved?

The setting supports this doubt—an ancient mansion, a family curse, mysterious events, and even attempted murder. The final part of the film combines religious ritual and medical treatment in an unusual but interesting way. The tantrik is shown as someone who respects science, and the psychiatrist is willing to work within the patient's cultural beliefs and myths. It may not be a realistic treatment model for real-life psychosis, but within the world of the film, it feels convincing.

Shobhana received both State and National Awards for Best Actress for her role as Ganga. Two dubbing artists, Bhagyalakshmi and Durga, voiced her Malayalam and Tamil dialogues. Shobhana's spoken Malayalam might not be strong, but her performance is still powerful. As Ganga, she is shy, soft, and gentle at first, but also has a dominating and fiery side that appears later. You can clearly see her transformation, and the climax is especially striking.

Suresh Gopi, who is usually known for loud action films and excessive English dialogues, surprises with a controlled performance. He plays a man who fears for his wife's life and also knows that her mental stability is at risk. Here, he feels more like a real person than a typical "hero."

Mohanlal, as Dr. Sunny, is naturally gifted as always. Some of his comic scenes feel overdone and a bit irritating, but when the story needs him to be serious and sharp, he is excellent. He can say a lot with just a small movement of his face.

The supporting actors are also strong. Nedumudi Venu, Innocent, Thilakan, and others are all dependable, and they deliver what Malayali viewers have come to expect from them. Vinaya Prasad, as Sreedevi, deserves special mention. She plays a woman who once had a crush on Nakulan and who now carries the burden of a "bad" horoscope. She is the quiet strength of the family, yet she is also the one people suspect. Without relying on long speeches, she brings out the pain of being judged and pitied.

Visually, the film uses space and light very well. Long corridors, dark corners, and half-seen figures increase the feeling of fear and tension. It is not a straightforward ghost story. Instead, it lets the audience's imagination create much of the horror. If you have ever listened to ghost stories from your parents or grandparents, the mood of this film will feel familiar.

The songs play a major role in telling the story. They are not just decorative; they carry clues and emotional hints. If you skip them, you actually miss information. M.G. Radhakrishnan's music, along with lyrics by Bichu Thirumala and Madhu Muttam, remains popular even today. While "Oru Murai Vanthu Parthaya" is the most famous track, "Varuvanillaarumee" and "Pazham Thamizh Paattu" are also beautiful and important to the narrative.

Psychosocial Analysis

It is true that the film has many psychological inaccuracies. But we have to remember the time it was made, the worldview of people then, and the kind of enjoyment the audience expected. If the film had depended only on scientific explanations, how many people would have liked it? For example, if Dr. Sunny had said at the very beginning, "Ganga is the mentally ill patient in Madampally—this is called dissociative identity disorder," then the film would have turned into a dull documentary, not an entertaining commercial success. The film works because it mixes science with entertainment—especially humor and suspense.

Ganga's transformation into Nagavalli and back is shown to take place in an abrupt way. In reality, patients with dissociative identity disorder do not change their identity in a split second. However, in the movie, during that brief moment of change between the two identities, Fazil captures the expressions, gestures, and body language very accurately. The audience, lost in the tension of the story, may not consciously notice it.

To keep the love for ghost stories and fairy tales alive, Dr. Sunny also takes the help of the tantrik, Brahmadatthan Namboothiripad. Because of this decision, the film became even more acceptable to a wide audience.

In reality, dissociative identity disorder cannot be cured fully by hypnotism alone; it needs long-term psychotherapy, counselling, medication, and other forms of support.

Director Brilliance

The film is a rich blend of psychology, folklore, witchcraft, and humor. In the beginning, the audience is completely convinced that there is a real ghost in the Madampally tharavadu. Fazil and his team manage to scare viewers without showing even a single actual ghost on screen. He achieves this through careful lighting, long empty corridors, quiet rooms, elements of village folk tales, symbolic scenes, and above all, Johnson Master's haunting background score.

Slowly, the film begins to move into psychological territory. Both explanations—supernatural and scientific—run side by side without clashing. Fazil keeps the viewer hooked from the first scene to the last.

Fazil's skill raises the film far above the level of a simple medical case study. His direction is like a textbook for students of Malayalam cinema. He did not just make a horror movie—he turned old folklore and superstitions into a full-length, enjoyable film experience, lifting them into the space of psychological entertainment.

Music

M.G. Radhakrishnan did not receive the National Award for the songs in the film, supposedly due to some technical reasons, even though he truly deserved it. The songs have now become part of Malayali cultural memory. Bichu Thirumala conveys the deep emotions of the characters—especially Nagavalli—through his lyrics without spelling everything out directly.

Johnson Master probably became the only composer who could frighten people using just the sound of the veena. That background theme has become iconic in Indian cinema.

Dr. Sunny Joseph

Dr. Sunny is one of the finest characters ever written in Malayalam cinema. Mohanlal plays him with a magical mix of humor, intelligence, medical understanding, and human warmth—often all in a single moment. He is a psychiatrist who tries not to hurt anyone. A genuinely kind man.

He gently pushes aside superstition. He stands for science, but without pride or cruelty. Through him, Fazil sends the message that mental illness can be treated with sensitivity, without shaming the patient. Here, mental illness is approached with humanity, not humiliation. Unlike many films of that time, Ganga is never shown as a villain, never mocked, never punished, and never stripped of her dignity.

Even with its scientific mistakes, this film still stands as one of India's best psychological thrillers.

A Different Perspective

A different interpretation by filmmaker Kalavoor Ravikumar is often discussed.

He once suggested that it was actually Nakul who was ill, not Ganga, and that Nakul was sexually impotent. He even met screenwriter Madhu Muttom to confirm his idea, and that interview was published in the film magazine Vellinakshatram.

Now, that reading has gained new relevance. In his own words:

"At that time, I was a trainee journalist at Kerala Kaumudi in Thiruvananthapuram. After watching Manichitrathazhu, I told editor Prasad Lakshman, 'Nakulan is not really interested in sex. The film is actually about Ganga's desire for Mahadevan, who lives next door.'

Prasad Lakshman did not dismiss me. He simply asked why I felt that way.

I became suspicious when I heard the song 'Varuvanillarum' from the film. This song was not written by the film's original lyricist. The script was written by Madhu Muttam the script writer.

Why did the writer take that risk? It felt like the hidden story was hidden inside that song.

The song says, 'Even though no one will come, I will wait with the door half open.' It suggests that there is no one in her life she can truly wait for with hope and care. Ganga's married life did not heal the loneliness of her childhood.

Ganga laments, 'I am an unblooming mango tree.' Perhaps the reason she has not had a child is tied to this feeling.

The names of the characters also seemed symbolic to me. Should Ganga be linked with Nakula, meaning 'one without a clan'? Or with Shiva? Isn't Mahadev another name for Shiva?

The relationship between Shiva and Ganga in mythology is not completely sacred—Shiva hides Ganga in his hair without Parvati's knowledge. In the film as well, Ganga's relationship with Mahadev is not sacred. She is shown embracing him during a festival night. She does many things to stop Nakul from discovering her passion for Mahadevan. She even tries to kill Alli, who hopes to marry Mahadev.

Even though Ganga and Nakul are newlyweds, we never see a single intimate moment between them. Nakul is always busy working in the bedroom. When Ganga asks if he wants to sleep, it is clearly an invitation for sex. Nakul refuses, saying he has work. Ganga asks him to call her when he comes to bed—another invitation. Still, Nakul refuses. Nakul is clearly a husband who turns down every approach his wife makes.

Once, during an interview with Fazil sir for a local channel in Alappuzha, I asked him if Suresh Gopi knew about this hinted affair.

He smiled and shook his head. 'No one knew.'

Watch Manichitrathazhu again. You will hear the scriptwriter's laughter and the director's laughter—loud and clear."

Dissociative Identity Disorder (DID)

This condition affects a person's personality, memory, awareness, and viewpoint—their entire way of experiencing the world. The main cause is repeated, severe psychological trauma in childhood, though not always.

To survive this pain, the person's mind creates another identity. The alternate personality is usually stronger, more confident, and emotionally healthier than the original.

Lack of attention and love, abuse within the family, natural disasters, war, kidnapping, and sexual assault can all contribute to this disorder. The second or third personality becomes a shield against trauma. When the pain surfaces, these other personalities take control. They may have different ways of speaking, different religious beliefs, different memories, different behaviour, and a completely different way of seeing the world. When these personalities are inactive, speech and behaviour switch back.

During these times, there may be a kind of amnesia that hides the true memories. In dissociative amnesia, a person may even forget who they are—a final attempt to escape unbearable pain.

Dissociative identity disorder is one of the most misunderstood illnesses. It is also called multiple personality disorder or split personality, but these terms are not accurate. Many people wrongly confuse it with schizophrenia.

There is also a common belief that people with DID are violent. In reality, they rarely hurt others. More often, they hurt themselves and become victims of other people's actions.

People think this disorder is easy to notice, but because it is so well hidden, only trained psychologists can truly recognize it. Films show personalities switching in a few dramatic seconds, but real cases usually shift much more slowly. In my professional life as a psychologist, I have seen the same kind of abrupt personality change in DID patients. But it often included acting as well. It is hard to realize the DID symptoms when they are mixed with acting. Some people think DID is "just acting only." But brain scans clearly show changes inside the brain during personality shifts.

Chapter 2

Oru Vadakkan Veeragatha

Directed by: T. Hariharan
Script / Screenplay: M.T. Vasudevan Nair
Music: Ravi Bombay
Cast: Mammootty, Suresh Gopi, Madhavi, Balan K. Nair, Captain Raju, Geeta, Sukumari

People say history is always written by the victor. What they often forget is that it is also twisted to favour the rich and the powerful. The history of North Kerala is also the history of the legendary Chekavars, masters of Kalaripayattu, one of the oldest martial arts in the world.

Stories of brave warriors and beautiful women exist everywhere. In Kerala, they took form as 'Vadakkan Pattukal' – the ballads of North Malabar. One such story is that of Aromal Chekavar, a 16th-century warrior, a name counted among the bravest of the brave. His life and death have been retold again and again, each generation adding its own layer, until it is hard to know where truth ends and legend begins.

In those days, among Nair clans, rich men often hired celebrated warriors to fight for them to settle disputes. Aromal is engaged to fight for a man locked in a property dispute with his own brother. In the duel that follows, Aromal's sword breaks at the hilt. When he accuses Chandu of treachery and claims that Chandu weakened his sword, Chandu kills his wounded cousin with a kuthuvilakku (a traditional oil lamp). Later, Aromalunni, Unniyarcha's son, finds Chandu and kills him. That is how the legend is usually told.

Chandu Chekavar (Chathiyan Chanthu)

Chandu Chekavar—also known as Chathiyan Chanthu or Chandu Panicker—lives in Kerala's memory through the old Northern Ballads, the Vadakkan Pattukal. These songs portray him as a sixteenth-century warrior from the famed Chekavar family.

Chandu- The Budding days

Chandu spent his childhood in the bustling Puthooram family home, growing up alongside his cousins Unniyarcha and Aromal Chekavar. It was there, under the watchful eyes of skilled Kalari masters—most importantly his uncle Kannappa Chekavar—that he learned the art of Kalaripayattu. Over time, the three children rose to become some of the finest fighters of their generation.

During his younger years, Chandu acted as the ceremonial groom for Unniyarcha in a 'Kettu Kalyanam', a mock wedding meant only as tradition. But Chandu misunderstood the ritual. He believed it was a true promise of marriage, something that would one day bind them together. That hope was crushed when both Unniyarcha and Aromal rejected the idea of such a union. Instead, she was married off to Kunjiraman of the Puthussery Kalari. From that moment, a slow-burning bitterness toward Aromal took root in Chandu's heart.

A chance for revenge arrived when the Puthooram family instructed Chandu to assist Aromal in a duel against the renowned warrior Aringodar. Chandu was given the responsibility of arranging Aromal's weapons. Secretly, he joined hands with Aringodar to prepare a faulty sword, believing it would guarantee Aromal's defeat.

But even with a damaged weapon, Aromal's skill prevailed. He managed to kill Aringodar, although he suffered minor injuries in the fight. Trusting Chandu completely, Aromal rested on his cousin's lap to regain strength. It was in that moment of vulnerability that Chandu finally acted—he pushed a lamp's metal wick-holder ('vilakku') into Aromal's wounds.

As he lay dying, Aromal told his family the truth about Chandu's betrayal. From that day on, Chandu earned the name 'Chathiyan Chanthu'—Chanthu the traitor.

Later, Chandu married Aringodar's daughter and inherited her father's property. His life continued, but the shadow of his actions stayed with him.

Years passed. Then the cycle of vengeance returned. Unniyarcha's son, Aromalunni Chekavar, met Chandu in an ankam—a formal duel—and ended his life, avenging his uncle at last.

MT Vasudevan Nair's Readings.

The story has been passed down countless times, but Malayalam writer M.T. Vasudevan Nair chose to tell it from a different angle – through the eyes of the man everyone loves to hate.

Set in the 16th century, the film begins when two young warriors arrive at Chandu's house and challenge him to a duel.

When Chandu (Mammootty) learns who they are, he is thrown back into memories of a past he has tried desperately to bury.

The Beginning

Kannappan Chekavar (Balan K. Nair) brings home the orphaned son of his estranged sister to Puthooram Veedu. The boy is kindly accepted by everyone in the house. Kannappan's daughter, young Unniyarcha, likes him immediately, but Aromal, the eldest son of the house, already on the edge of manhood, treats him with scorn. Little Chandu prays with all his heart that one day his name too will be sung in heroic ballads. (It is a beautiful scene, because we, the audience, know that his wish will indeed come true—but not the way he imagines.)

As Kannappan begins to train both his own children and his nephew, he is amazed by how quickly Chandu absorbs the family's martial art. Aromal is annoyed to see this "urchin cousin" rise so swiftly in his father's eyes. Unniyarcha, however, is drawn to Chandu's gentle nature and gives him an affection that soothes his starved heart.

The tension between Chandu and Aromal (Suresh Gopi) only deepens as they grow into adults. Aromal's fame spreads as he wins tournaments across the land. Chandu, less showy, chooses to stay in the background, deferring to his famous cousin—partly out of respect for his skills, and partly because he is deeply grateful to his uncle. Kannappan, however, knows his nephew is the better warrior and tells him so, much to Aromal's annoyance. This praise for Chandu only widens the gap between the two young men.

The affection between Unniyarcha (Madhavi) and Chandu grows slowly into love.

However, Aromal's dislike of Chandu has only hardened over the years. He takes it upon himself to give Unniyarcha's hand to Kunjiraman (Sreeraman).

To make everything worse, Kunjunooli (Chitra), another young woman who openly shows her interest in Chandu, is married off to Aromal instead.

Heartbroken, Chandu leaves Puthooram and travels to Tulunad (present-day Karnataka), where he trains under Aringodar (Captain Raju), a Kalari master of great repute.

Back home, Unniyarcha's love for Chandu has not faded. When she hears that her husband will be away one night, she secretly sends a message, calling Chandu to meet her. Blinded by love, Chandu does not hesitate. He rides through the night on horseback, crosses raging waters, and finally reaches her.

But fate intervenes—Kunjiraman returns unexpectedly. Terrified for her honour, Unniyarcha cries out, pretending that Chandu is attacking her.

Cornered and humiliated, Chandu has no choice but to flee. That one night leaves him with a new shameful title—'pennmohi' (lecherous) Chandu.

Crushed by what he sees as a double betrayal, Chandu returns to his guru and buries himself in training. One day, a feudal lord comes to Aringodar seeking help in a property war with his cousin. The dispute is to be settled through a duel between champions. As destiny would have it, the landlord's cousin goes to Puthooram and begs Aromal to fight for him.

Kannappan Chekavar is restless. He knows that Aringodar has far more battlefield experience than Aromal. He also knows his own son's flaws—a quick temper, an impulsive mind. Unlike Chandu, for whom the sword is like an extra limb, Aromal wields his weapon as just that—a weapon. Kannappan offers to fight for the naaduvazhi (local ruler), but when the ruler hesitates, he tells him to find another mercenary. Aromal, arriving at that moment, eagerly accepts the offer and demands a huge fee for the honour. Worried for his son, Kannappan begs Chandu to act as Aromal's aide. Chandu is torn—on one side is the uncle who gave him a home; on the other, his guru.

Unniyarcha tips the scales. She promises Chandu that if he stands by her brother and they return victorious, she will leave her husband and become his wife, even if Aromal objects. No one, she says, will be able to blame her for keeping that promise. For Chandu, it is as if the gates of heaven have opened. He agrees.

As Aromal's second, Chandu takes his cousin's swords to the blacksmith to be reforged and sharpened. But Kunji (Geeta), Aringodar's daughter, is terrified for her father's life and jealous of anything that might draw Chandu away from her. She bribes the blacksmith to weaken Aromal's sword by placing a wooden rivet inside the hilt instead of a metal one.

The duel begins. Aromal's command of swordplay is excellent, but Aringodar's experience slowly starts to overpower him. At a crucial moment, Aromal's sword breaks in the middle of the battle. Chandu, as his second, asks for a pause so he can replace the weapon. Honour rules the 'ankathattu' (the duelling platform), and Aringodar, respecting those rules, agrees. He turns away, weapons lowered. At that instant, Aromal hurls the broken sword into his back and kills him.

Chandu, shattered, returns to camp, only to be greeted by a storm of accusations. Aromal, wounded and furious, accuses him of treachery of the worst kind. A fight breaks out. Weakened, Aromal stumbles, trips against the lamp, and falls onto it, fatally wounded.

News of Aringodar's death travels fast, and people rush to congratulate Aromal. Instead, they find the bloodied warrior dying in Chandu's lap. His last words are bitter and final: "Chandu chathichu" (Chandu betrayed me).

Chandu escapes from the raging crowd and hunts down the blacksmith, who confesses that he weakened the sword under Kunji's orders. Filled with despair and fury, Chandu storms into Aringodar's house, only to discover that Kunji, upon hearing of her father's death, has already hanged herself.

Now Chandu has nowhere left to go. He returns to Puthooram, where he faces Unniyarcha again. Her brother's death has burned away all her love. In its place stands a fierce, lifelong hatred. She swears that her son will one day avenge Aromal.

"I swear my unborn son will avenge his uncle's death." (She really does swear a lot.)

Years pass. Now Aromalunni (Unniyarcha's son) and Kanappanunni (Aromal Chekavar's son) have come to keep that promise. The night gives way to dawn; Chandu is still hesitant to fight two inexperienced boys. They refuse to back down. Aromalunni insists he cannot return without Chandu's head—he gave his mother his word.

Chandu is broken too. Aromalunni could have been his son, if fate had not twisted his life. He cannot bear the thought of Unniyarcha's son losing in battle. His love for her has remained, buried but alive, all these years. In the end, he chooses the only path he sees—he sacrifices his own life, ending the game fate has played with him.

We watch this entire tale through Chandu's eyes and are left with a strange uneasiness. Perhaps there is more to the story than we grew up hearing. Perhaps he was not the coward he is always made out to be. Perhaps he deserves pity more than blame. Like another tragic hero, Karna from the Mahabharata, maybe Chandu too is a man crushed by destiny.

Psycho Social Analysis

Oru Vadakkan Veeragatha is undoubtedly one of the finest classic films ever made in Malayalam. It has an extraordinary script written by one of the greatest Malayalam writers, Jnanpith Award winner M. T. Vasudevan Nair. With this film, MT's magical pen changed "Chathiyan Chandu" – a name that once meant "cheat" in the northern ballads – into a symbol of a misunderstood man in the minds of Malayalis.

In Shakespeare's play 'Julius Caesar', Brutus gives a speech just after Caesar is killed. He convinces the Roman crowd that Caesar, though his dear friend, was a dictator who deserved to die. Then Mark Antony rises to speak to the same crowd, the same people who had just cheered the assassination. After Antony's speech, the crowd turns against

Brutus and Cassius, who had killed Caesar.

You can compare MT's script to Mark Antony's speech. Malayalis began to embrace the once-despised Chathiyan Chandu and Aringodar Chekavar, who had always been portrayed as villains. At the same time, they began to dislike Aromal Chekavar and Unniyarcha, who until then had shone brightly in the songs of the Panars.

Everyone who dared to make a film like this deserves special praise. Especially M. T. Vasudevan Nair's wonderful script, which raised a completely lowly character like Chathiyan Chandu into a powerful, lasting memory in Malayali minds. The dialogues shine like a silver line—nothing more, nothing less. Hariharan's unmatched direction, his skill in choosing the right actors, producer P. V. Gangadharan, who had the courage to invest heavily in bringing a character seen as the symbol of evil into the light of goodness, and to question beliefs that had existed for generations—all of them deserve appreciation.

The film was enriched by the art direction of K. Ramachandrababu. The music, composed by K. Jayakumar, Kaithapram Damodaran, and Bombay Ravi, and the songs sung by K. J. Yesudas and K. S. Chitra, became etched forever in the hearts of the people of Kerala.

The film won four National Film Awards and eight State Awards, including Best Actor (Mammootty), Best Screenplay (M. T. Vasudevan Nair), Best Production Design, and Best Costume Design (P. Krishnamurthy).

Let us take a closer look at the characters.

Chandu's Childhood and Youth (Vineeth, Mammootty)

When we look at the characters, it's interesting to remember that Mammootty was considered the very symbol of male beauty in that era. Yet in this film, while every other character appears polished, Mammootty is kept deliberately plain. Because Chandu is a man without charm, without the ease of privilege. His father, a poor man who struggled even for daily needs, is killed in battle by a Malayan for a small fee. Chandu is left alone in a home that reflects nothing but poverty. When both his parents die, he truly has no place to go.

But like Shakespeare, M. T. Vasudevan Nair never writes anyone as completely good or completely evil. There is no flawless hero here, and no villain filled with only darkness.

Chandu's uncle, Kannappa Chekavar, brings him home. And unlike the usual stories of orphans, Kannappa's wife also accepts him wholeheartedly. Chandu enters the Puthooram household—a place alive with joy, prosperity, and abundance. To him, it feels like a magical world he had never imagined. Yet, deep down, he never feels he belongs there.

His first thoughts as a child rise from that very courtyard: *"Children who learned to play chess with gold coins in their pockets... but the nameless Chekavar's son never felt it was his home."*

Everyone treats him with love—Unniyarcha, her younger brother Unnikannan, and the rest of the family. But Kannappa Chekavar's eldest son, Aromal, dislikes Chandu from the very beginning.

Chandu falls in love with Unniyarcha at a very young age.

Their child marriage, their Kalari training, and their life under the same roof only deepen that love. But without Chandu even realising it, Unniyarcha's marriage to Kunhiraman is being arranged.

Unniyarcha's abandonment shatters Chandu.
He says, *"My desire, my meditation, the love that entered my mind like a frenzy from the age of thirteen—everything was lost."*

There is also Kunjunnooli, who falls in love with Chandu. Though he rejects her at first, the pain of Unniyarcha's betrayal pushes him towards her. He goes to Kunjunnooli's home with a marriage proposal. But by then, Kannappa Chekavar has already arranged a match—for Aromal Chekavar.

Aromal Chekavar (Suresh Gopi)

Aromal Chekavar is believed to have lived in the 16th century in the North Malabar region of present-day Kerala. Known as 'Puthooram Veettil Aromal Chekavar', he was the elder brother of Unniyarcha and the uncle of Aromalunni—both renowned warriors in their own right.

His story lives on in the 'Puthooram Pattu', a set of ballads from the larger tradition of 'Vadakkan Pattukal'—the Northern Ballads of Kerala, composed during the 17th and 18th centuries. These songs celebrate the spirit of 'vira', the heroic mood: tales filled with courage and sacrifice, beauty and stubborn pride, glamour and goodness.

In the film, Aromal is portrayed as a proud, fiery man. He is an exceptional martial artist—brilliant, sharp, and skilled. Yet even at his best, he is never truly above Chandu.

Aromal often mocks Chandu openly and behind his back. To him, Chandu is just a wanderer—someone with no noble lineage, no family wealth, no name. He considers himself superior in every way, including in Kalari skills. And when he realises that Chandu and his sister Unniyarcha love each other, it is Aromal who arranges her marriage to his wealthy friend Kunhiraman.

But even with all this arrogance, Aromal is not written as a one-sided villain. He is brave—deeply brave. He never backs away from danger. His father, Kannappan, looks at him with a kind of proud admiration. Aromal steps into battle with the unbeatable Aringodar Chekavar without fear.

When he tells his brother,
"When I am here, our family should not have the shame of sending our father to die in battle,"
he means every word. He knows he may die at Aringodar's hands. That is why he demands enough money from the ruler—not for himself, but to feed three generations of his family if he falls.

Kunhiraman (V. K. Sreeraman)

In the old northern ballads, Kunhiraman is often portrayed as a coward—weak, useless, and lacking any real skill in battle. But in M. T. Vasudevan Nair's script, he is reshaped into a far more grounded and respectable character.

Kunhiraman is practical. He knows Kalaripayattu, and he has courage—just not the reckless kind. He understands how to earn a stable living by starting Kalari schools and teaching students. He is neither weak nor incapable. Unlike many warriors of his clan, he does not gamble his life for a single payment and die in some arena for another man's glory.

He also marries the most beautiful and gifted woman of the region—Unniyarcha. While the ballads depict him as an old man, the film shows him as only slightly older than Unniyarcha, his graceful and talented wife.

Unniyarcha (Madhavi)

Unniyarcha belonged to the famed Puthooram Veedu of Kadathanad (Vadakara) in northern Kerala. Throughout her life, she was lovingly called 'Puthooramputhri'—the daughter of the Puthooram household. After her marriage to Kunjiraman, she was also known as 'Attummanammel Unniyarcha'. Her husband ran a Kalari called Puthussery Kalari, which, according to legend, still exists in the Kannur district today.

Stories say that Unniyarcha won *sixty-four* Kalari ankams in her youth. She was the sister of Aromal Chekavar and Unnikannan. She famously rejected the love of Chandu Chekavar, a decision that would later lead Chandu to betray her brother Aromal. Years later, her son Aromalunni avenged his uncle by killing Chandu.

One of the most dramatic episodes in the Northern Ballads is the 'Nadapuram Fight', which takes place soon after Unniyarcha's marriage to 'Attummanammel Kunhiraman'. Unniyarcha wished to attend a series of local festivals, but the path she had to take was unsafe. The Mappila (Jonaka) men in the Nadapuram bazaar were feared by everyone. Her husband and relatives begged her not to travel—but Unniyarcha refused to be intimidated.

As warned, Unniyarcha and Kunhiraman were ambushed at Nadapuram. Kunhiraman froze in terror, but Unniyarcha, fearless and skilled, drew her sword and fought fiercely. The headman of the Mappilas, initially stunned by her beauty and intent on taking her captive, soon realised who she was—the sister of Aromal Chekavar, a warrior he deeply respected.

He, along with the local chieftain's wife and an influential Chetti, pleaded for her forgiveness and offered gifts. But Unniyarcha refused to lower her sword. She demanded one thing: a solemn promise that no woman would ever again fear harassment or attack while travelling that route.

Only after securing this powerful assurance—a vow of safety and dignity for all women—did Unniyarcha finally make peace.

The casting of Unniyarcha deserves special praise. Madhavi brings the character to life with a rare, striking beauty—her eyes, her posture, her effortless grace. There is something almost serpentine about her presence, a beauty that feels dangerous and irresistible at the same time. It is the kind of beauty that can wound, the kind that lingers long after she leaves the frame.

It is difficult to imagine anyone other than Madhavi playing Unniyarcha. She is, in every way, unforgettable.

MT's Unniyarcha – A Woman Who Lives by Her Own Rules

In MT's version, Unniyarcha is portrayed as a woman with extraordinary courage and an unshakeable sense of self. She decides for herself, stands firm in her choices, and has little interest in pleasing society or following old customs. We see this clearly through Kunjunnooli's sharp observations.

When Chandu remarks, "A woman should not enter the Kalari when the Chekavar is in meditation," Kunjunnooli responds, "But Unniyarcha walks in whenever she wants.

Does she have her own set of rules?" Chandu is left speechless. Later, when Kunjunnooli tries to be close to him and he hesitates, saying, "We must behave properly," she challenges him again: "Then why doesn't Archa think like that?"

What do these small moments reveal?
First, Unniyarcha is not someone who quietly obeys others or lives in fear of anyone.
Second, no one in her family controls her. She follows her own heart and does not care about gossip or traditions.

Even after her marriage, Unniyarcha deliberately tries to draw Chandu back into her life. She calls him to her room when her husband is away, and when she is nearly caught, she places the entire blame on Chandu and slips away without consequence. When Kunhiraman reaches for his sword in anger, she stops him with calm authority—fully aware that if a fight begins, Kunhiraman may lose his life. Nothing about this behaviour is innocent.

She tempts Chandu again. She pleads with him—now a disciple of Aringodar who knows every trick of his master—to help Aromal in the upcoming duel between Aringodar and Aromal. She promises him that if her brother survives, she will become his wife.

When Chandu asks, "Aren't you carrying a child now?", she answers, "Let my father and brother return the wedding thread. I will tell them this was the vow I made when my brother went to battle." Her words only pull Chandu deeper into longing.

At this point, the audience naturally wonders: "If she had such boldness, why didn't she marry Chandu earlier?"

Unniyarcha herself explains it. She says that even though she married into a wealthy family, she is not living like a queen. She is not covered in gold ornaments. She has endless chores. She cannot enter the Kalari, nor can she practice martial arts. So, although she agreed to the marriage for the sake of wealth and status, she now lives almost like a servant.

When she admits, "I only wanted to bear your child and raise my old lover's child without anyone knowing," we realise that her intentions cross moral boundaries that no society would accept.

Finally, when she sends her own son and son-in-law to kill Chandu—going directly against her father's wishes—we must conclude that Unniyarcha has lost her moral compass entirely.

In the end, Unniyarcha goes ahead with her decision to send her son and son-in-law to kill Chandu, even though her father would never have supported such an act. By doing this, she shows that she has lost all sense of morality.

When Chandu asks her son, *"Did your mother not warn you about coming after a man who will cut you down without hesitation?"* listen to the boy's reply:
"She told me that killing you with my own hands would bring honour to our house."
She even blessed him for it.

This shows the state of Unniyarcha's mind. She knows Chandu Chekavar cannot be defeated easily, and she knows her son is not fully trained. Yet she pushes him forward with words soaked in pride, not truth.

Kannappa Chekavar (Balan K. Nair)

Kannappa Chekavar brings his orphaned nephew Chandu into his home with genuine affection. He trains him in the art of Kalaripayattu and even gives his own daughter to Chandu in a child marriage. There is not the slightest sign of discrimination from him; he stands by Chandu in every possible way.

In one scene, Kannappa says that Chandu's movements were better during the demonstration fight. Chandu answers softly, "That is enough for me. I need nothing more." That single reply shows how deeply Chandu valued his uncle's approval.

Yet, it is difficult to believe that this same Kannappa later yielded to Aromal's wishes and married his daughter to Kunhiraman instead. Kannappa is strong-willed in every other matter; there seems to be no reason for him to bow before his son only on the subject of Unniyarcha's marriage.

So why did he change his mind?
Was it the fear that his daughter would gain nothing by marrying a man with no wealth?
Or did the bright promise of Kunhiraman's riches cloud his judgment?

This is the same Kannappan who chooses a wealthier family for Aromal's marriage, favouring Kunjunnooli's household over Thumbolarcha's. But once the wedding takes place, Aromal begins an affair with Thumbolarcha anyway. Their relationship even leads to a child. Strangely, no one in the Puthooram home seems troubled by this behaviour.

Kannappa also shows no moral hesitation when he tells Chandu to serve as Aromal's assistant in the duel against Aringodar—Chandu's own teacher. Everyone, including Unniyarcha, pressures Chandu to help Aromal. Aromal himself adds an insult: "Even you will do." Yet no one—not even Chandu—questions whether this is unfair to Aringodar.

Toward the end of the story, Kannappan's anger and thirst for revenge against Chandu grow fierce. He says, "He betrayed me. I let him sit on my lap, I raised him, I never imagined he would deceive me." Then he adds, "When you cut off his head, tell him this is a special Kalari strike blessed by our ancestors."

These words reveal how completely Kannappa forgets the love he once had for Chandu. After Aromal's accusations, not Kannappan, not Unniyarcha, not Kunjunnooli, not even Unnikannan—who is little more than a quiet presence in that old house—tries to find out what actually happened in the duel with Aringodar or how Aromal truly died.

Kunjunnooli (Chithra)

Kunjunnooli's life is shaped by a soft, unspoken sorrow. She moves through each day carrying the memory of her forgotten love for Chandu, while quietly enduring her husband's betrayal. In the Puthooram household, she receives neither affection nor warmth. She remains unseen, uncared for—yet she never protests.

She is a woman who absorbs every wound in silence.

And finally, in that same silence, she gives her quiet consent to Unniyarcha's thirst for revenge. In the end, Kunjunnooli even takes part in sending her son and son-in-law to kill Chandu—the very man she once loved with all her hear

Aringodar Chekavar (Captain Raju)

Aringodar Chekavar stands out as one of the most unforgettable figures in 'Oru Vadakkan Veeragadha'. In many ways, he is the only character who can truly claim unwavering honesty, fairness, and fearless strength.

He never allows anyone to break his rules—his discipline, his sense of right and wrong, or his straightforward truth. People whisper that he knows magic, illusions, and even charms strong enough to control an elephant. But Aringodar never hides behind tricks. He never forces anyone into silence.

He does not show special favour to any disciple. When Chandu comes to learn from him, Aringodar tells him plainly, "There is nothing left for you to learn except what the great Kannappa Chekavar has already taught you." He disarms Chandu without even lifting a weapon and adds, "Now perhaps you understand that Aringodar does not rely on magic or deception."

Aringodar carries himself with a dignity and seriousness that dominate every scene. Even Mammootty—known for his commanding presence—fades slightly beside Captain Raju's towering performance.

Even when he discovers that Chandu is assisting his enemy Aromal, Aringodar stays calm. He simply says, "Yes, he is your cousin. It is your duty to stand with him." Meanwhile, his own students cry out that this is betrayal, but Aringodar never once loses his poise.

When he hears that Aromal will face him in the duel, Aringodar remarks, "I thought Kannappa Chekavar himself would come. I always wondered which of us was the better fighter. That question remains unanswered."

He openly mocks the petty quarrels and customs of the land. To him, these fights are meaningless—battles over the throne of a fish or the seeds of a jackfruit. "As a Chekavar, is my life meant only to kill or be killed for someone else? That is the fate of a Chekavar—to die or to take another's life in service of another man's dispute."

Even though he knows his daughter cares for Chandu, and even though he senses that death is approaching, Aringodar never suggests that Chandu should marry her. When he asks Chandu, "Didn't you choose me as your teacher as well? Tell me, whose victory are you praying for now?", Chandu remains silent—but Aringodar expects nothing more.

In truth, Aringodar never realises that Chandu is helping Aromal because Chandu believes Aromal's victory will finally win him Unniyarcha.

Chandu (Mammootty)

At the heart of the film stands Chandu—a man shaped by his vulnerabilities more than his strengths. During the most difficult phase of his life, it was Aringodar Chekavar who took him in with kindness and treated him like a true student. Yet Chandu has no hesitation in standing beside Aromal in the duel against Aringodar—his own beloved master—despite Aromal being the very man who mocked him and shattered his trust.

Chandu keeps falling for Unniyarcha's words, again and again. It is painfully unfair that he chooses Aromal's side even after learning every sacred technique from the great Aringodar. Unniyarcha, who has betrayed him repeatedly—and is now married and carrying her husband's child—still succeeds in pulling Chandu into her web of promises. And he allows himself to be deceived once more.

During the duel, Aringodar clearly begins to overpower Aromal. But Chandu, overwhelmed with anger and confusion, shouts his master's name and physically restrains him. The look on Aringodar's face in that moment says everything:
Chandu, how could you do this? How could my own student betray me?

It is a silent echo of Caesar's final disbelief— 'You too, Brutus?'

When Aringodar stops fighting and stands without a weapon, Aromal commits the gravest betrayal: he hurls the broken sword and kills Aringodar in cold blood. Chandu sees this—he knows every rule of honour has been broken—yet he feels no guilt, no grief, not even a flicker of regret.

Instead, Chandu tells Aromal, "I needed to win this war more than you." For Chandu, nothing mattered—not loyalty, not justice, not the life of his master. The only thing he cared about was winning Unniyarcha, even if others had to die for that desire.

Kunji (Geetha)

Kunji, Aringodar's daughter, is one of the most heartbreaking figures in the film. She knows her father is walking toward his death, and she knows she will be left completely alone when he falls. She also understands that her father will never ask Chandu to marry her, even though she loves him deeply.

When Kunji learns that Chandu—the student who should have stood by her father—has chosen to fight on Aromal's side, her pain turns into anger. She lashes out at him, saying that Unniyarcha knows she can beat him with a broom, walk away, and he will still crawl back the moment she calls. Stung by her words, Chandu slaps her.

Kunji immediately apologizes. She pleads with him, telling him that her father is waiting for a single word from Chandu—hoping he will accept his daughter. But Chandu's heart belongs entirely to Unniyarcha, and nothing Kunji says can touch him. She begs him to speak just one word: 'agree.' Instead, Chandu diverts the conversation, avoiding her hope.

Terrified for her father's life, Kunji secretly bribes the blacksmith to weaken Aromal's dagger, hoping it will save Aringodar. But fate does not bend for her. Aringodar is killed.

Then comes the final cruelty—Chandu goes to kill Kunji, the daughter of his own guru, the woman who loved him without reservation. With every last hope shattered, Kunji chooses to end her life.

Chandu Chekavar (Mammootty) — The Final appearance

In the end, the story returns to the opening flashback, and we see Chandu rise once more with quiet strength. He has now become the master of eighteen Kalaris. This part of the film contains one of Mammootty's finest performances.

Aromal's son and Unniyarcha's son arrive to kill him. Chandu tries again and again to send them away, teasing them by saying they are still boys who do not even know the basics of Kalaripayattu.

He declares with pride, “No man can defeat Chandu in open combat with weapons and armour.” But beneath those words lies a deep wound—the pain of knowing that his own uncle, the man he once loved above all, has sent assassins after him. Chandu is fully aware that he has nothing to prove to these teenagers. If he wished, he could slice them apart in moments. He could even take revenge on Unniyarcha herself.

From the beginning, Chandu has said he wishes to see no one. He is exhausted from living as “Chathiyan Chandu”—the most despised traitor in legend—carrying a life of loneliness and disgrace. Now only Kuttimani remains beside him in the Kalari. It is to Kuttimani that Chandu tells the whole story of his life—the story that forms the heart of the film.

Chandu is a man eternally misunderstood, a man who failed in every relationship and every emotion. Above everything else, he was consumed by his obsession with Unniyarcha—and because of that, he could never truly love or desire another woman.

At last, Chandu raises his sword and turns it upon himself. He ends his life so that his long journey of being misunderstood can finally stop. He asks that people begin singing the praises of Aromalunni, the son of Unniyarcha, instead of cursing his name forever.

And when he tells Unniyarcha’s son, “You are the son I never had,” we understand that his love for Unniyarcha never died. It lived within him until his final breath.

Kutti Mani

Kutti Mani, the daughter-in-law of Aringodar Chekavar, is the only person who remains with Chandu until his final moments. She says that Chandu Chekavar never once harmed her—that he showed her nothing but kindness and affection. And in the end, like Chandu, she is left with no one of her own.

Performances and Craft

Mammootty is perhaps India's finest actor when it comes to subtle expression and voice modulation. Madhavi communicates emotions through her eyes in a way few actresses can match. Captain Raju, Balan K. Nair, and Geetha bring depth through the smallest gestures—never relying on unnecessary movements.
'Oru Vadakkan Veeragatha' is not only a milestone in Malayalam cinema, but a masterclass for all of Indian cinema.

When Pain Becomes Entertainment

In ancient Rome, people filled the Colosseum to watch humans and animals tear each other apart, enjoying the horror as entertainment. In some Tamil Nadu villages, crowds cheered during cockfights and bullfights. But in Kannur—the land of warriors—people watched human beings fight each other directly. Men entered duels knowing they might not walk out alive, and the crowd roared when one of them fell and died.

Sadism

There is a psychological condition where a person feels pleasure when another suffers. In some individuals, this feeling becomes extremely intense. Such people may inflict violent torture for enjoyment.

There are psychopaths who bite or cut their partners during sex, tie them to beds and whip them, shock them with electricity, slice their skin with blades, mutilate their bodies, and even kill them—deriving sexual pleasure from their pain. This tendency to enjoy the suffering of others appears in different degrees across society.

In psychology, this pattern of behaviour is called 'sadistic personality disorder'.

Oru Vadakkan Veeragatha offers a powerful exploration of how society creates its heroes and villains—not through truth, but through stories repeated for generations. The film shows how honour, reputation, and family pride can twist human behaviour, turning small weaknesses into lifelong tragedies.

Through Chandu's character, the film examines loneliness, rejection, emotional manipulation, and the deep human need to belong. It shows how a misunderstood man becomes a symbol of betrayal simply because society needs someone to blame.

The movie also reflects the rigid social rules of the time: caste hierarchy, expectations placed on men and women, and the harsh warrior code that demanded loyalty even when it destroyed humanity.

In this way, the film becomes more than a retelling of folklore—it becomes a mirror, revealing how easily society judges without understanding.

Chapter 3

Thaniyavarthanam

Directed by: Sibi Malayil
Written by: A. K. Lohithadas
Produced by: Nandakumar
Starring: Mammootty, Thilakan, Mukesh, Saritha, Philomina, Kaviyoor Ponnamma
Music:
Score: Johnson
Songs: M. G. Radhakrishnan

Thaniyavarthanam (English: The Repeating Rhythm) is a 1987 Malayalam psychological drama written by A. K. Lohithadas and directed by Sibi Malayil. The film stars Mammootty as schoolteacher Balagopalan, Thilakan as the powerful uncle of the matrilineal family, Mukesh as Gopinathan, and Kaviyoor Ponnamma as Balagopalan's mother. The film became a cult classic. Thilakan won the Kerala State Film Award for Second Best Actor.

A Landmark Release

When the film was released, it received widespread critical praise. It explored superstition and rigid orthodoxy in rural Kerala, society's harsh treatment of people with mental illness, the clash between old traditions and new ideas, and the slow breakdown of once-proud Nair joint families. Even today, Lohithadas' screenplay stands out for its scientific accuracy and its honest portrayal of psychological pressure.

Birth of a Great Movie

Let me share a small story.

Director Sibi Malayil once told Mammootty that a young man was coming to narrate a story. At that time, Lohithadas was not famous, not even recognised as a major writer. Mammootty was very busy and not in the mood to listen. He did not even offer Lohithadas a chair. Standing at the door, Mammootty said, "Tell me quickly, I'm a bit busy." He agreed to listen only because Sibi insisted.

Lohithadas began narrating the story from the very beginning. He had no real hope—Mammootty looked clearly uninterested. But halfway through the narration, something shifted. Mammootty stopped him, invited him inside, asked him to sit, and told him to continue the story.

When Lohithadas finished, Mammootty sat quietly for a moment, thinking. Lohithadas, worried that he might face criticism, got up to leave. But Mammootty asked him, "Who is going to write the script for this?"

Lohithadas replied, "We haven't decided yet… we need to find someone."

Mammootty said, "No. You should write it yourself."

Lohithadas hesitated. "I've never written a script before."

Mammootty responded, "You narrated it beautifully. You must write it yourself."

And that single moment became the beginning of one of Malayalam cinema's greatest screenwriters—and the birth of one of its most celebrated classic films.

Plot

The House That Remembers

The story takes place inside a large, ageing Nair tharavadu—a quiet ancestral home where Balagopalan Mash, a government school drawing teacher, lives with his wife, mother, two children, younger brother Gopi, and younger sister.

Gopi, played by Mukesh, is young, educated, and strongly opposed to superstition. But the elders of the house hold tightly to old beliefs and rigid customs. Mammootty's character, Balan Mash, also lives under this same suffocating system.

In this family, the 'karnavar'—the eldest maternal uncle—holds absolute authority. Just as tradition dictates, it is the uncle who takes every major decision, not the father. Thilakan plays this dominating great-uncle with powerful command.

Another uncle lives in the house—Sreedharan, played by Babu Namboothiri. He is believed to be mentally unstable and is kept chained inside a dark room. Years ago, an elder from the family had thrown the idol of Bhadrakali from the Malankara temple into a well. People believe the goddess cursed the family, dooming one man from every generation to madness. Sreedharan is seen as the latest victim of that curse. Everyone believes that once he dies, the curse will finally be lifted, and the goddess will forgive them.

The Violence of Belief

In one corner of this vast ancestral home sits Cheriyamma, played by Philomina—a woman who spreads superstition like wildfire.

Gopi warns the family that unless they sell the property and leave, none of them will survive. But no one listens. He even says Sreedharan should have been taken to a mental hospital years ago instead of being chained like an animal, and that euthanasia would have been kinder than this prolonged suffering. The family refuses. They hide behind the excuse of the *curse*.

The younger sister's marriage gets cancelled because the groom's family refuses to marry into a "cursed" lineage. When Gopi says that idols and deities are valued more than human lives in this house, it hits a painful truth. Even today, in many parts of India, innocent people are killed over cows.

Gopi tells Cheriyamma, "You won't let anyone escape this curse," and he is right. The family clings to the myth, trapping themselves in fear. In reality, Sreedharan may have suffered deep trauma after his wife's death, but instead of help, he was labelled mad and imprisoned for life.

Imagined Fate, Real Consequences

One night, Balagopalan quietly unchains Sreedharan and lets him step outside. By the next morning, Sreedharan is found dead in the ancestral pond. After twenty-four years in darkness, he finally finds release.

The villagers immediately begin whispering:
"Who will go mad next—Balan Mash or Gopi?"

Sreedharan's death shakes Balagopalan deeply. The following night, he has a violent nightmare and wakes up screaming, suddenly frightened that the curse may not have ended. Word spreads quickly through the village. Everyone connected to Balan begins to look at him with suspicion.

At first, he denies it and tries to defend himself. But when even his students begin doubting him, the pressure slowly breaks him. Gopi's warning becomes true—everyone is waiting for the next victim.

Balan feels like an outsider at his own sister's wedding. His wife and children go back to her home. When he goes there to bring them back, her family refuses to let him in. Hurt and frustrated, he reacts emotionally—and that single moment is enough for everyone to label him "completely mad."

The family locks him in the same dark room where Sreedharan was once chained. A prophecy becomes reality. A curse becomes a self-fulfilling tragedy.

Redemption

In the end, the same mother who fed him his first grain of rice gives him his last meal. She mixes poison into his food, feeds him, and then eats the same food herself. Her final act is both love and despair—a desperate attempt to end her child's suffering.

This entire tragedy is not the fault of one person.
It is the cruelty of a whole society trapped in fear, superstition, and generational ignorance.

Psycho-Social Analysis

Stigma and Collective Fear

The film shows how mental illness is misunderstood in traditional communities—feared like a plague, whispered about like a curse.

Madness becomes a stain that no one wants to touch.

Balagopalan's downfall begins with a tiny fear inside him. But that fear grows because everyone around him feeds it. The worried faces of his family, the frightened voices of the villagers, the stares, the gossip, and the old beliefs trap him. Slowly, he stops trusting his own thoughts. Society's fear becomes his own—and that shared fear destroys him.

Self-Fulfilling Prophecy

A self-fulfilling prophecy happens when a prediction pushes people—knowingly or unknowingly—to make it real. Sometimes the person who predicts it drives it forward; sometimes the person who believes it does.

When someone believes something strongly, that belief itself directs their actions.

This can help in life, but it can also ruin a life.

These prophecies appear in families, friendships, and society. Once a prediction is made about someone's nature or future, people behave in ways that push that prediction toward reality.

Example:
A lizard falls on you in the morning.
You think, 'This is bad luck. Today will be terrible'. Even if you tell your wife it will be a good day, your mind stays restless. You magnify problems, ignore small joys, lose patience easily, and react sharply. Others respond to your irritation.
By evening, the day truly becomes bad.

Your belief created the outcome.

The Myth of Bloodline

Many cultures believe mental illness is inherited—a curse flowing through family blood.

Yes, some conditions do run in families. But mental illness is far more complex than a simple genetic chain.

The real tragedy begins when illness is treated as a curse instead of a medical condition.

In the film, the grandmother's chanting, the mother's tears, and the neighbours' whispers all arise from the same fear—the belief that madness belongs to their bloodline. This fear becomes an excuse.
It allows the family to avoid compassion, responsibility, or professional help.
Superstition becomes the easiest explanation for every suffering.

The Collapse of Identity

Balagopalan's fall from a confident teacher to a trembling man is not caused by mental illness; it is caused by the slow destruction of his confidence.

Every step he takes, every pause he makes, even his silence is treated as proof of madness. He is watched constantly, doubted endlessly and eventually, he begins doubting himself.

This is "socially created mental illness." Society breaks him long before illness does.

Mammootty portrays this collapse with chilling accuracy—the fear in his eyes, the trembling in his voice, the quiet panic hidden in his words. His world collapses quietly, and no actor could have shown it more truthfully.

Panopticon / Panopticism

Panopticism explains how constant watching—or the belief of being watched—controls human behaviour.
French philosopher Michel Foucault wrote about it in ***Discipline and Punish*** (1975).
The idea comes from Jeremy Bentham's Panopticon—a circular prison with a central tower. The guard can see every prisoner, but the prisoners cannot see the guard. Not knowing when they're watched, they discipline themselves.

Just like how people behave more cautiously when CCTV cameras appear.

In ***Thaniyavarthanam***, this invisible watchtower is the entire village. Everyone watches Balagopalan—family, neighbours, colleagues, even children.
Every blink, every gesture, every word is interpreted as madness.

This constant surveillance shatters his peace. He begins living as if a thousand eyes follow him. And that slow pressure breaks him.

The Diathesis–Stress Model

The Diathesis–Stress Model explains why some people develop mental illness while others—facing the same struggles—do not.

Two forces must meet:

Diathesis: The inborn vulnerability or psychological sensitivity.
Stress: A life event or pressure so heavy that the mind cannot carry it.

When vulnerability meets overwhelming stress, illness can appear.

Think of diathesis as a seed. It stays quiet unless the right conditions make it grow.

This is why some people with a family history never fall ill, while others do. In Balagopalan's case, the family history becomes the diathesis—his inherited vulnerability. The superstition, stigma, fear, and pressure around him become the stress.

His mind breaks not because he is weak, but because the society around him crushes him.

Society Induced Madness

This film is not about one man going mad.
It is about how an entire community pushes him toward madness.

Balagopalan is not born insane. He sees himself through the terrified eyes of the people around him— until he becomes exactly what they expect him to be.

That is why 'Thaniyavarthanam' remains such a powerful and painful experience. It shows how families and societies can break a human being without realizing it.

Unlike gaslighting—where manipulation is intentional—here, the destruction is caused by superstition, ignorance, and fear. Lohithadas tells the story of a man who accepts madness because society leaves him no other choice.

Chapter 4

Bhoothakkandi

Bhoothakkannadi, meaning *Magnifying Glass*, is a Malayalam psychological drama released in 1997. Written and directed by A. K. Lohithadas in his very first venture as a filmmaker, the movie traces the troubled inner world of Vidyadharan, played with quiet power by Mammootty. A simple clockmaker by trade, Vidyadharan finds himself unable to face the cruel turns of life, and his fragile mind slowly begins to crumble under the weight of fear, guilt, and misunderstanding.

Although the film did not perform well at the box office, it soon grew into one of the most respected works in Malayalam cinema. Critics praised its depth, its emotional honesty, and its striking portrayal of psychological collapse. Lohithadas received the Indira Gandhi Award for Best Debut Director at the National Film Awards, and the film was honoured with the Kerala State Film Award for Best Film in 1997. It also secured two Filmfare Awards South, along with the Padmarajan Award for Lohithadas's remarkable screenplay.

Plot

The story begins inside a prison cell, where Vidyadharan sits alone, serving his sentence. The reasons that led this gentle watch-repairer to such a bleak place unfold slowly, like the gears of a clock turning one by one, revealing the tragedy of a man who lost his way in the shadows of his own mind

Mammootty plays Vidyadharan, a simple watch and clock repairer. His fears begin in childhood. One day, while returning from school, he and his friends spotted a snake on the road. They threw stones at it. One snake was struck on the head and died. Vidyadharan became convinced that a second snake moved toward him—seeking revenge for its dead companion.

From that moment, a deep fear took root inside him. He believed that one day, the surviving snake would return.

Years later, his wife dies from a snakebite. Vidyadharan becomes completely certain that the same snake had come back to kill her out of vengeance. After her death, he never walks outside without carrying a torch, terrified of what might be hiding in the dark.

Living nearby is Sarojini, his childhood friend and first love. Her marriage lasted only one night—her husband abandoned her and never came back. She now raises her teenage daughter alone, carrying the weight of loneliness and social judgment.

Ophiophobia

Because of his deep fear of snakes, Vidyadharan walks through the village with a torch—even under bright daylight. His unusual terror is unmistakable. This intense, irrational fear of snakes is known as 'ophiophobia or ophidiophobia'.

His only daughter, Sreekutty, is the center of his world. Vidyadharan raises her with immense love. He also cares for Minikutty—Sarojini's daughter—as if she were his own child. The film beautifully captures rural life, along with the fears and beliefs that shape that world.

Minikutty grows into a beautiful young woman. One day, she suddenly goes missing. The whole village joins the search. Eventually, her body is found inside a cave near the mountain. The police report says she was gang-raped. After this tragedy, Vidyadharan's life is shattered.

He insists that the crime was committed by a drunken man who often wandered around with a gun. This man had troubled Sarojini's family before, but he had no real link to the murder. The police arrest him, interrogate him, and eventually realize he is innocent.

But Vidyadharan refuses to believe this. In his mind, the man is guilty. During a heated fight, the man dies, and Vidyadharan is arrested.

Life in Prison

Inside the prison campus, Vidyadharan leads a quiet life and becomes the warden's favourite. Sarojini visits him regularly, but his daughter has been taken away by her mother's family.

During one visit, Sarojini tells him she met Sreekutty and that she has grown into a young girl. Vidyadharan longs to see her, but he is told her family will never allow it. That same day, Sarojini talks about the rising number of assaults and molestation cases in society, reminding him of what happened to Minikutty. These stories disturb Vidyadharan deeply—especially because his own daughter is now entering the same dangerous world.

As his release date approaches, Vidyadharan dreams of a peaceful future. He tells Sarojini that he wants to take her and his daughter far away and start a new life. He asks her to convince her family and bring his daughter to him. Sarojini promises she will.

Vidyadharan grows happier day by day. During his afternoon walks, he discovers a tiny hole in the thick prison wall. Curious, he clears it and uses his magnifying glass to look through. To his shock, the hole goes right through the wall, giving him a clear view of a hilltop outside. Amazed, he keeps this secret to himself—especially because freedom is so close.

The Illusion

Through the hole, Vidyadharan watches a small blind family living on the hilltop. He listens to their songs and watches their simple life. But he also notices something disturbing: a constable from the jail keeps troubling them, forcing them to move. Inside the prison, Vidyadharan meets the same constable but cannot express his anger. He remembers the man's rude behaviour during Sarojini's visit and becomes convinced he is dangerous.

One day, Vidyadharan sees the blind family celebrating—their young daughter has reached adolescence. This makes him think of his own Sreekutty, now the same age.

But soon he witnesses something horrifying. The constable enters the hut when the girl is alone. Moments later, Vidyadharan hears her screams. She runs out, chased by the constable like a wild animal. Vidyadharan shouts for help, but no one hears him. Trapped behind the walls, he watches helplessly.

When the blind parents return and discover what happened, their grief is unbearable. They set fire to their hut and burn themselves alive. Vidyadharan watches it all in silence, broken and powerless.

The Collapse

The next morning, during routine inspection, the same constable stands before the inmates. By now, Vidyadharan has completely lost control. He attacks the man, crying out that he destroyed three innocent lives. The warden and prisoners pull him away. Vidyadharan shows the hole in the wall and explains everything he witnessed.

The jailer checks the wall. There is no hole, only solid brick. Everything Vidyadharan saw was a creation of his wounded mind.

The Final Blow

Later, Sarojini arrives with Sreekutty. Vidyadharan looks at them with empty eyes. When they step closer, he turns away and asks, “Aara?”— “Who are you?”

The film ends with an aerial view of a train pulling out of the station—a haunting symbol of a life that has slipped away forever.

Psychosocial Analysis

The Fixation and the Breakdown

Vidyadharan, a modest watch and clock repairer, finds his world collapse inside the prison walls. One day, after he vomits his food, the jailer confronts him, shouting, “You won’t eat and will not allow others to eat!” This phrase instantly triggers a deep trauma in Vidyadharan, as the ‘exact same words’ were once spoken by the drunkard he killed. The potent similarity causes Vidyadharan’s mind to immediately identify the jailer as a sexual molester. He looks through the cell wall and experiences terrifying hallucinations: he sees the jailer sexually assaulting a teenage girl and setting fire to the blind couple's home. During this terrifying vision, he sees his own daughter mixed into the scene. Furthermore, he begins to see the jailer not as a new man, but as the actual hunter he had killed in an earlier confrontation. Consumed by this distorted reality, Vidyadharan violently attacks the jailer.

The prison superintendent, who genuinely cares for Vidyadharan, investigates the violent outburst and quickly discerns his troubled mental state. Subsequently, Vidyadharan is formally diagnosed with a mental illness and transferred to a hospital. The story reaches its agonizing emotional peak when Sarojini finally arrives at the hospital, bringing his daughter with her. At this moment, Vidyadharan's mental condition fractures completely, and in a devastating tragedy, he asks, 'Who are you?'

Fixed Ideas

While the clinical term **fixation** in classical psychology originates with Freud's theory of psychosexual development, the concept of a "fixation to an idea" connects to several specific mental concepts that describe an overly rigid or obsessive attachment to a single thought. This attachment is always pathological and intense.

In the case of 'Obsessive-Compulsive Disorder (OCD)', fixation manifests as an 'obsession'—a constant, intrusive, and unwelcome idea, image, or urge that generates deep anxiety and distress. Conversely, in severe conditions like 'schizophrenia' or delusional disorder, this fixation hardens into a 'delusion'—a fixed belief that is entirely detached from actual reality.

Schizophrenia and Distortion

From childhood, the initial trauma of the snake incident made Vidyadharan believe the creature held a permanent grudge against him. Over time, this singular belief grew exponentially, eventually driving him into a state resembling schizophrenia.

Schizophrenia is one of the most complex and widely misunderstood conditions of the human mind. It is a state where the ability to distinguish between what is real and what is illusion is severely compromised. For observers, the affected person's entire world appears to have shattered. This disorder profoundly alters how a person thinks, feels, and experiences life.

It is like viewing existence through a broken, scattered lens. All sensory input—voices, images, thoughts, and emotions—becomes warped and disconnected.

Science has not yet found one exact cause, but several medical theories exist for schizophrenia. The disorder is consistently linked to abnormalities in brain structure and chemistry. Chemical messengers (neurotransmitters) like dopamine, glutamate, serotonin, GABA, and acetylcholine often fail to function correctly. Structural differences are sometimes noted in areas like the hippocampus, thalamus, and prefrontal cortex. Other contributing factors include genetics, severe childhood stress, infections, or drug use during critical stages of brain development.

Schizophrenia affects about 1% of the world's population. It is a severe and long-lasting mental health disorder. Individuals living with schizophrenia often seem disconnected from reality, causing emotional pain not only for themselves but also for their families. It is vital to note that a common misconception is that schizophrenia is the same as Dissociative Identity Disorder (DID) or "split personality"—it is not.

Symptoms

Symptoms can include hearing voices that aren't physically present, seeing things that do not exist, or holding intense beliefs completely disconnected from reality—such as thinking someone is constantly watching them or believing they possess godlike powers. This condition can also disrupt speech, causing it to become disjointed or illogical. In Vidyadharan's case, the incident where he hears a child crying inside the jail is a 'hallucination'. Hallucinations are sensory deceptions generated by the mind that manifest through sight, sound, taste, touch, or smell. Hearing or seeing things that are unreal fall into this category.

Cinematic Excellence

Boothakannadi is one of those rare films that once experienced, your mind will not allow you to rewatch it casually. Vidyadharan was a complex character carefully created by Lohithadas, and Mammootty embodies the role with piercing intensity on screen. This film stands as a remarkable demonstration of Mammootty's natural acting genius, with the climax sequence widely regarded as one of the best performances of his acting career. Sreelakshmi delivered a powerful portrayal of the character Sarojini. Indeed, in this movie, every single actor, with utmost brilliance, executed their characters beautifully.

Chapter 5

Jawan of Vellimalai

Jawan of Vellimala is a 2012 Malayalam film written by James Albert and directed by first-time filmmaker Anoop Kannan.

Mammootty plays Gopikrishnan, a pump operator working at the Vellimala Dam. He once served in the Army but had to return home because of a mysterious health issue. Neither he nor the villagers know what that illness truly is. Gopi's father died fighting for the dam, and Gopi himself has fought in the war—but even after all this, the villagers remain dissatisfied with him.

At night, Gopi sees the spirits of people who died near the dam—figures only he can see. Everyone else thinks he is simply scared or weak. They mock him and question whether he was ever a real soldier.

But Gopikrishnan is not a coward. He is extremely brave. None of these ghosts harm him. He believes that if anyone else had seen such terrifying visions, they would either lose their sanity or end their life.

Haunted by wartime memories, sleepless nights, the eerie silence around the dam, and unhealed psychological wounds, Gopi suffers silently. Mammootty portrays his inner turmoil—PTSD, loneliness, and fear—with remarkable depth.

The rest of the plot follows familiar "dam story" clichés—corruption, mismanagement, an honest engineer fighting the system, and villainous officials. A cartoonishly evil Chief Engineer and several unnecessary characters weaken the film.

It is only at the end that we discover the real reason only Gopikrishnan can see ghosts. The truth comes out when he meets an ophthalmologist.

The Actual Illness: Charles Bonnet Syndrome

Charles Bonnet Syndrome (CBS) usually appears in older adults, especially those with conditions like 'macular degeneration, glaucoma', or other forms of major vision loss. People with CBS see vivid visual illusions even though they are fully awake and mentally sound.

Around **20–30%** of people with severe vision loss experience this condition.

They may see:

- flames
- children
- people
- distorted or frightening shapes
- figures sitting on their bed

These visions can appear incredibly real, yet the person may still know they are not true.

CBS occurs because the brain refuses to accept the lack of visual input. When clear images fail to reach the brain due to damaged eyesight, the brain "fills in the blanks" with its own creations—producing vivid hallucinations.

A medical journal once reported the case of a seventy-eight-year-old priest who said he saw distorted figures dancing inside his Bible. His eyesight had become very poor. Once he wore proper glasses and read in good lighting, the hallucinations reduced drastically.

Psychosocial Analysis

The Silent Wounds of a Soldier

Gopikrishnan comes home from the Army carrying wounds no one can see. The memories of war remain alive in him—shadows that visit him at night, sudden jolts of fear, and an inner restlessness he cannot name. He is haunted not by the battles he fought, but by the ones he survived. These signs point to the quiet torment of trauma, yet the villagers see only one thing: a soldier who returned early. Their judgment becomes a heavier burden than the war itself. The world outside misreads everything happening inside him, and that painful gap becomes the heart of Gopi's suffering.

2. The Cost of Masculinity

In Vellimala, a man is expected to be unshakable. Fear is seen as weakness, and vulnerability is not allowed. When Gopi admits he sees visions, the villagers quickly brand him as fragile. Their ridicule comes not from truth but from rigid beliefs about what a man should be. Gopi is not harmed by the ghosts he sees; he is harmed by the shame placed upon him. The harshness of these expectations leaves no space for tenderness or understanding. In such a world, a man breaks not because he is weak, but because he is not permitted to bend.

Final Thoughts

Jawan of Vellimala carries a meaningful idea at its core, but the screenplay struggles to hold its emotional weight. The writing does not always meet the depth of the subject, yet the film still offers a sensitive look at how trauma, misunderstanding, and rigid social beliefs shape a person's life. It invites us to pay attention to the quiet wounds people carry and teaches us the importance of responding to pain with compassion rather than judgement.

Despite its flaws, the film remains important because of how it portrays Gopikrishnan's inner world. His journey shows how easily society can misread a wounded soul and how urgently we need empathy, awareness of conditions like Charles Bonnet Syndrome, and a kinder understanding of masculinity. Mammootty's performance lifts the character from the page and fills him with dignity, vulnerability, and quiet strength. Through him, the film becomes a touching exploration of human fragility—and a gentle call to be kinder to those who suffer in silence.

Chapter 6

Aham

The Pretence of Care

The film opens inside an ashram that claims to care for people with mental illness. The place is run with tenderness, and a middle-aged Christian nun watches over everything. The residents wander freely, and their behaviour is often shown through humour. But as time passes, it becomes clear that no one in this ashram ever improves. Their suffering is presented almost like entertainment, turning serious conditions into moments of laughter.

Men with long-standing delusions, frightening hallucinations, obsessive rituals, and deep depression live there without a single form of treatment. There is no doctor, no trained nurse, and no structured medical care. They simply exist—unhealed and unnoticed. Siddharth, played by Mohanlal, also carries intense delusions and depression, yet the delusions that once shattered his life strangely disappear once he enters the ashram.

Everyone there calls Siddharth "Swami." He dresses like a monk and mixes ideas from the Bible, the Quran, and the Bhagavad Gita into his own personal philosophy. The mother superior's niece, Mariana, arrives from America to study this unusual man.

As a psychologist, I often wonder what is truly so exceptional about Siddharth that demands such "special research." Mariana, played by Ramya Krishnan, approaches him with warmth and curiosity. Her closeness awakens emotions that

Siddharth had long buried.

The rest of the film unfolds from the story Mariana hears from Dr. Menon, the psychiatrist who once treated Siddharth.

The Slow Destruction

Siddharthan grows up in a large ancestral home filled with people yet empty of affection. His mother keeps her distance, and his father is a stern judge who values rules more than relationships. The only tenderness Siddharthan knows comes from the family steward and the steward's children. They are the only ones who make him feel seen.

Then comes the moment that crushes his childhood. His father sentences the same steward—the only man Siddharth loved—to death. For Siddharthan, this is not justice; it is a deep and unforgivable betrayal. Something inside him shatters. From that day on, he cuts his father out of his heart and grows up as a lonely soul in a house that never offers warmth.

Trauma-Driven Perfectionism

Siddharthan grows into a man who believes that controlling every detail of life will protect him from hurt. As a bank manager, he clings to strict rules—fixed office hours, tidy routines, and a need for perfect order. He avoids tea, coffee, or alcohol, drinks only milk, and boils his egg for exactly forty-seven seconds.

This obsession with neatness is not a sign of discipline; it is the language of fear. Fear of chaos. Fear of losing control. Fear of the world outside him.

Psychology calls this pattern Obsessive–Compulsive Disorder (OCD), shaped by a childhood ruled by his father's harsh authority and his mother's emotional absence.

Trapped by Doubt

Renjini tries to build a life with him, but the more she reaches outward, the more anxious Siddharthan becomes. When she begins helping at her father's friend's shop, he cannot bear it. His fear deepens when she reconnects with an old classmate who is now an Army officer. What begins as simple friendship turns, in Siddharthan's mind, into a story of betrayal.

His thoughts grow darker, sliding into paranoid patterns similar to Paranoid Personality Disorder. This slowly transforms into a condition known as Othello Syndrome—a delusional belief that one's spouse is unfaithful. Their home becomes a battleground where fear speaks louder than love.

The Night of Collapse

During one argument, Renjini slips from the stairs and falls into a coma. Siddharthan is devastated. He spends long nights at the hospital, unable to face the truth of what has happened.

It is during this vulnerable time that he meets his former lover, Vimala. Around her, his strict routines soften. He finds comfort in her presence, as if she is the last safe place in a collapsing world. Their bond grows close again, and she becomes pregnant.

Hallucinations to Collapse

Yet truth eventually reaches him. Siddharthan discovers that Renjini never betrayed him. The gift she bought for him was paid for by her father's friend, not through any wrongdoing. This discovery tears him apart. His guilt becomes too heavy to carry.

As he walks toward Renjini's hospital room with this burden pressing on him, he begins hearing her voice inside his head—hallucinations urging him to kill Vimala. Unable to separate reality from despair, he begs Vimala to abort the pregnancy. When she refuses, the hallucination grows stronger.

In that unstable moment, Siddharthan kills her.
When he returns home, he learns that Renjini has died as well.
Every fragment of sanity inside him breaks.

The Spiritual Mask

Now mentally unstable, Siddharthan is admitted to a hospital and later moved to an ashram that treats illness with sympathy but no science. There are no doctors, no therapy, and no medication—only storytelling, prayer, and emotional care.

Here, Siddharthan takes on saffron robes and slowly becomes "Siddhartha Swami." The residents treat him with reverence, but beneath the spiritual mask is a man crushed by guilt and grief, trying to hide inside silence.

Mariana- His Last Hope

Into this fragile world arrives Mariana, the Mother Superior's niece who has come from America to "study" mental illness. The film never explains what exactly she hopes to discover, making her work seem more symbolic than scientific.

Mariana treats Siddharthan with warmth and patience. Her presence awakens old needs inside him—the longing for affection, the ache of loneliness, the fragile hope of being understood. For a moment, he feels alive again.

But when Mariana gets married, he collapses emotionally. The only small hope he had disappears. Unable to bear this new emptiness, he ends his life.

Siddharthan's life is a tragic journey shaped by a wounded mind. His behavior reflects:

- attachment trauma from a cold, loveless childhood
- obsessive patterns born from fear and rigid discipline
- paranoid jealousy that destroys his marriage
- hallucinations triggered by guilt and emotional collapse
- a fractured identity that hides behind spirituality
- a desperate hunger for human connection
- a loneliness so deep that it leads to suicide

The film attempts to speak about mental illness but ends up sending troubling messages—that spirituality can replace medical treatment and that emotional suffering heals through faith alone.

Even so, Mohanlal and Urvashi deliver extraordinary performances that lift the story above its flaws. They give Siddharthan's tragedy a depth and tenderness that linger long after the film ends.

Chapter 7

Nine

Many Malayalam films have explored the human mind with remarkable sensitivity. ‘Nine’ is one of them—a film rich in psychological depth—yet it slipped past the audience, unnoticed and misunderstood.

Failure at the Box Office

The first reason lies in the way the story is presented. The ideas are layered, several moments feel unclear, and the film occasionally dips into science fiction. Even though Kerala values scientific thinking more than most Indian states, science-fiction thrillers have rarely succeeded here.

The second reason is its non-linear narration. The movie jumps between timelines without warning, making it difficult for the average viewer to find a stable thread. Many felt lost long before the emotional core revealed itself.

The third reason is its lack of commercial elements. The film carries psychological and social themes, rich with detail, but it offers little humour or entertainment. Its seriousness became its weakness in the market, though beneath that surface waits a deeply insightful story about the mind.

Paternal Distance, Silent Child

Dr. Albert Lewis, a widowed astrophysicist, lives in Kerala with his young son, Adam. He is brilliant, respected, disciplined—and emotionally closed. Albert still carries the pain of losing his wife, Annie, during childbirth. A quiet corner of his heart blames Adam for her death.

Annie's brother shares the same bitterness. His own son was paralysed in an accident that happened while playing with Adam, and he now believes Adam brings misfortune wherever he goes.

Adam grows into a withdrawn, sombre child—sensitive, lonely, and misunderstood. His small misbehaviours irritate Albert, who responds with coldness rather than empathy. For Adam, his father is the only world he has. For Albert, the boy is both love and fear—love he cannot express, fear he cannot face.

Solitude as Reflection

Hoping to bond with his son, Albert moves to an old bungalow in a remote mountain village—a place without electricity, phones, or the comfort of modern life. The silence of this new world is unsettling. When routine disappears, Albert's mind—already heavy with grief and guilt—begins revealing what he has tried to bury.

The darkness around him becomes symbolic: villages that once feared ghosts lost those fears after electricity arrived. Here, in absolute darkness, Albert's mind begins creating ghosts of its own.

Old Wounds Return

In this lonely setting, Albert's past comes rushing back. Memories of Annie's death, his silent blame on Adam, and the roughness with which he treated the boy all rise to the surface. Soon, he begins hallucinating—wolves on the hillside, strange figures in the shadows, and visions of Annie.

At the same time, a mysterious girl appears in his life—a figure the viewers first mistake as supernatural. But the truth is far more human. She is not a spirit, not an alien, not a visitor from another planet. She is a creation of Albert's own mind—a psychological projection. In reality, she does not exist.

Ava is the shape of Albert's broken emotions.

When Ava comforts Adam, Albert is actually being kind. When Ava grows violent, it is Albert who harms the boy. Albert insists that Ava is attacking Adam, but the child senses the truth—his father is losing control.

A Mind Lost to Fear

Meanwhile, villagers create their own mythology around Albert's behaviour. They speak of a cursed nine-day period, evil forces, and strange events. They believe Adam has attacked people and spoken in an unknown language. Tribal groups accuse Albert of beating one of their own. Albert denies everything and blames the comet he found in the forest.

He convinces himself that he is defending the world from an alien threat. What he cannot do is face his own child. His unresolved fears make reconciliation impossible.

Ava, in reality, is Albert's dissociated self—one version of him loving, another version harming. His condition resembles dissociative identity disorder, shaped by trauma and guilt.

Symbols That Speak

Adam

A picture of innocence. The only person Albert truly loves, yet the one he fears hurting most.

The Comet

A trigger that unlocks Albert's buried pain.

Ava

A living shadow of Albert's guilt, loneliness, and unhealed grief.

The mountains and the darkness

A reflection of Albert's inner emptiness.

Albert's battle in Nine is never with extraterrestrial beings. It is a battle with himself—his memories, his fears, his guilt, and the truths he has avoided for years.

Misdiagnosis

In the film, a doctor tells Albert he has "bipolar schizophrenia," a term that does not exist in clinical practice. The closest accurate diagnosis would be schizoaffective disorder, bipolar type—a condition where mood swings blend with hallucinations and delusions.

Despite these flaws, 'Nine' remains a film with a powerful emotional core and a thoughtful script. It reminds us that the most terrifying battles take place inside the human mind. As the film suggests:

"*The monsters we fear most live in the corners of our own thoughts.*"

Chapter 8

Mukundan Unni Associates

Mukundan Unni Associates is a 2022 Malayalam dark-comedy crime film directed by Abhinav Sunder Nayak, starring Vineeth Sreenivasan, Suraj Venjaramoodu, and Aarsha Chandini. The film earned strong critical praise and became a commercial success.

Mukundan Unni is a struggling lawyer obsessed with becoming wealthy. Despite his rigid discipline, his career keeps failing. When his mother breaks her leg, he cannot afford her surgery. An insurance fixer steps in and helps him fake the incident as a road accident to claim money. Through this, Mukundan discovers how lucrative insurance scams can be—and he quickly dives into the racket.

Before long, he conflicts with Venu, the very man who taught him these tricks. When Venu blocks him from getting clients, Mukundan takes a brutal step: he plants a cobra in Venu's car, causing Venu's death. With his rival gone, Mukundan widens his scam empire without hesitation.

A forged medical report soon puts him at legal risk. Terrified, he even considers suicide. But his attempt indirectly triggers a terrible bus accident involving 31 schoolchildren. Immediately, Mukundan sees profit in the tragedy. He begins filing compensation claims for every victim.

Around the same time, the judge handling his case is suspended after fake documents—planted by the hospital owner—are found on his laptop. The path ahead clears for Mukundan. He then sabotages the hospital's power and ambulance service, ensuring the injured children cannot be transferred elsewhere.

His associate Robin tries to blackmail him, but Mukundan crashes the car, leaving Robin brain-dead. When a child dies due to negligence, Mukundan manipulates the hospital into handing him control of the entire institution.

By the end, Mukundan has everything he dreamed of—absolute control over the hospital and the insurance-claim business—built on lies, staged accidents, and calculated cruelty.

Psychosocial Analysis

The story follows an unemployed lawyer who, desperate to pay for his mother's surgery, turns to illegal ways of earning money. Once greed takes hold, he stops at nothing. Vineeth Sreenivasan plays Mukundan Unni, a character who leaves it to the audience to decide whether he is the hero or the villain.

This is one of the most meticulously written scripts about a psychopath—precise, scientific, and chilling. Unlike films about serial killers or sociopaths, this one portrays a victorious psychopath who outsmarts society at every turn. He manipulates everyone, gloats openly, and wins. Directed by Abhinav Sunder Nayak and written by Vimal Gopalakrishnan along with Nayak, the film deserves immense credit for its psychological depth. It opens boldly with the title card: "No Thanks to Anyone." Psychopaths walk among us every day, and the writers capture their thinking with alarming accuracy.

In today's world, if we look closely, we will see these personalities everywhere. The film leaves a heavy feeling, a reminder of the society we live in. With better attention to casting and certain production choices, the movie could have been a massive mainstream hit.

Narcissistic and Anti-Social Traits

Mukundan Unni never tolerates resistance. He does not explode with anger; instead, he quietly removes anyone who obstructs him.

Lack of Empathy

Death does not disturb him. He even views tragedy as an opportunity for profit. He feels no guilt, no regret.

Mukundan is skilled at drawing people close when he needs them. He behaves gently, speaks politely, and shows perfect self-control. He turns every person, every accident, every disaster, and every death into a stepping stone for his own success.

This man—whether you see him as villain or hero—looks harmless, speaks sweetly, and appears emotionally stable. He never behaves impulsively. He is sharply focused and entirely driven by his goals.

Modern Corporate Evil

The film is not merely about one man's cruelty. It reflects a wider corporate culture built on ambition and greed. These individuals are competent, modern, and ruthless. They are experts at exploiting loopholes and manipulating systems. The hospital staff, doctors, lawyers, and clients around Mukundan are not innocent—they are parts of a corrupt machine. Mukundan is simply the most efficient hunter among them, coordinating the entire chain of exploitation.

This mirrors the corporate world, where confidence and success are rewarded, and morality rarely finds a place. Mukundan rises because:

- people admire his determination
- clients fall for his smooth speech
- authorities rarely question a man who appears successful
- others participate due to their own greed

The film becomes a mirror held up to society, exposing our hypocrisy.

It also reveals an uncomfortable truth: many viewers secretly enjoy Mukundan's cunning moves. They laugh, feel thrilled, and almost celebrate his cruelty. Why do we admire someone so immoral? Because society values confidence, intelligence, and success—even when wrapped in evil. This is exactly how real life works: corrupt people often win, honest people often fail, and shameless individuals manipulate systems effortlessly.

The Dark Triad of Personalities

Psychology groups certain destructive personality traits into what is called the Dark Triad:

Psychopathy

People imagine psychopaths as violent criminals, but many are calm, rational, and socially skilled. They understand their actions—they simply do not feel the emotional weight of those actions. Newer research even suggests that psychopathy can be reduced or treated.

Narcissism

Narcissists carry extreme selfishness, deep insecurity, and a constant need for admiration. They cannot tolerate criticism and often seek revenge for even small insults.

Machiavellianism

Not a mental illness, but a personality pattern marked by manipulation, deceit, and a lack of concern for others. Many such individuals live among us.

As Yudhishthira tells the Yaksha, the mental state in which one thinks “nothing bad will happen to me even when everyone around me is dying” mirrors how these dark personalities function.

The Just-World Phenomenon

This theory suggests that people believe the world is fair—that good deeds bring rewards, and bad deeds bring punishment. Because of this belief, people tend to blame victims. When tragedy strikes, society searches for reasons to justify the event.

People assume:

- victims must have done something wrong
- success must reflect good character
- failure must reflect personal flaws

Research shows a strong link between just-world beliefs and religiosity.

This mentality is why society often blames:

- the poor for their poverty
- victims of sexual assault for their clothes or behaviour

Why It Happens

People fear confronting the randomness of life. By blaming victims, they imagine they can avoid similar fate. It helps them feel safe in a chaotic world.

Back to Mukundan Unni Associates

The script does not present just one bad person. Everyone around Mukundan carries their own moral cracks. This is the true picture of society. As the Stanford Prison Experiment demonstrated, people can turn into angels or devils depending solely on circumstance. The film suggests that individuals are not born good or evil; behaviour is shaped by situation and pressure. Mukundan and the people around him exploit law and power with frightening ease.

The final line spoken by Meenakshi rejects the comforting belief that karma always delivers justice. That belief itself is born from cognitive biases such as wishful thinking and the just-world hypothesis, which allow people to feel safe even when reality offers no such guarantee.

In the ancient episode of Yaksha and Yudhishthira, the story pauses not on power or victory, but on awareness. When the Yaksha asks what is most surprising in the world, Yudhishthira replies that people witness death every day, yet live as though they are exempt from it. His answer cuts through time. It reflects the deeper truth that wisdom lies not in strength or knowledge, but in humility before impermanence. Life continues because the mind quietly denies its own end, and it is this gentle self-deception that allows humans to hope, act, and survive, even while standing in the shadow of certainty.

This same pattern appears in society. People deny danger even when it surrounds them. They assume misfortune belongs to others, not to themselves. This mindset protects us from constant fear, but it also blinds us to reality. Even as society begins to collapse, people continue living as if they are safe.

A Final Thought

Mother Teresa once said that forgiveness is difficult, yet necessary. Doing good is hard, but even the smallest act of kindness can light another person's world. In a narrative filled with cold ambition and cruelty, this message becomes a gentle reminder of the humanity we must not lose.

Chapter 9

Innale

Innale (Yesterday), released in 1990, is a Malayalam psychological drama written and directed by P. Padmarajan. The film features Suresh Gopi, Jayaram, Shobhana, and Srividya in the lead roles, with music composed by Perumbavoor G. Ravindranath and Mohan Sithara.

I can still hear, in memory, the radio advertisement that played when the movie first came out. "A bus has overturned in the hilly village of Thampuran Kunnu. Only one young woman survives—she cannot remember her name or the place she came from. Her story… the story of her forgotten yesterdays… Padmarajan's 'Innale', presented by AVR Productions." Then came the gentle tune of the theme song. When I watched the film as a teenager, the purity of its love story touched my heart like a cool breeze.

Shobhana plays a woman who survives a bus accident but loses every trace of her past. She cannot recall her name, her home, or anything she once knew. Dr. Sandhya, played by Srividya, treats her at the hospital. While staying in their home, she receives a new name—Maya. In time, Maya falls in love with Dr. Sandhya's son, Sarath Menon, played by Jayaram.

But the peace in her new life begins to shake when people from her former world arrive looking for her. Suresh Gopi appears as Dr. Narendran, a man searching for his wife, Gauri.

Maya, however, does not recognize him. Narendran sees at once that she is indeed his wife, but she no longer carries him in her mind. Understanding that she now loves Sarath, he quietly steps back and says she is not his wife anymore.

Amnesia:

Padmarajan introduced the Malayalam audience to amnesia with a tenderness and imagination that felt new and deeply emotional. Viewers were drawn to Shobhana's character, a woman who forgets her own name and must slowly rebuild herself in ***Innale***.

Stories about men or women who lose their memory after an accident have fascinated film lovers everywhere. Hollywood has used this idea many times in films like *The Garden of Lies* (1915), *Santa Who* (2000), *The Bourne Ultimatum,* and *The Long Kiss Goodnight.* All of them revolve around the strange and haunting world of amnesia.

Beyond Cinematic Amnesia

Amnesia can occur after a head injury, a stroke, or as a side effect of certain medicines. There are several forms of memory loss. When a person cannot recall past events, it is called 'retrograde amnesia'. They may lose their entire history, yet still learn new things with no difficulty.

In 'anterograde amnesia', the opposite happens—they struggle to remember new events, names, or conversations. They may read the same page or meet the same person again and again as if for the first time. Yet their older memories remain clear.

Cinema also popularized the magical idea that a second blow to the head can restore lost memory. Many still believe this, especially in North America, where 38–46 percent of people think a second injury can undo the first. In reality, this is impossible. A second trauma only increases the chance of further damage.

Psychogenic Fugue

Psychogenic fugue is a rare condition that appears after emotional shock or psychological trauma. These individuals forget who they are and lose all sense of identity. The stress may come from mental illness, emotional crisis, or unbearable life situations. Some recover quickly; others leave their homes, travel far away, and live under a completely new identity.

The Strange Case of Ansel Bourne

Ansel Bourne (1826–1910) was an American preacher and carpenter. In January 1887, he suddenly left his home in Rhode Island. Without understanding how or why, he reached Norristown, Pennsylvania.

There, he began living as a man named J. Brown. He opened a small shop selling stationery and sweets and lived quietly for six weeks. He had no memory of his earlier life or who he truly was.

Then, one day, everything returned. He saw a “Missing” poster with his own name on it—and at that moment, his forgotten life came rushing back. Psychologists studying his case noted that fugue states can appear without warning and may end suddenly through a trigger—something familiar, like a sound or a face. For some people, the memory comes back gradually; for others, it never returns.

Returning to the movie

The scene where Dr. Narendran arrives in search of his wife is one of the most emotional moments in the film. While watching it, almost everyone wishes that Maya will not recognize him, because by then her heart belongs to Sarath. Narendran knows she is his Gauri, yet he chooses to walk away. If you were in Dr. Narendran's place, what would you have done? I have asked many people, and most have no clear answer.

He recognizes her. He realizes she is living as someone else, in another man's love. And he leaves her behind. Was he right to do so?

Think of it this way: years pass. Maya may now be a happy wife, perhaps even a loving mother. The loss of her earlier life is no longer a wound. But one day, an old song, a familiar book, a forgotten scent, or a face from the past might break open her memory. Everything she once knew could return suddenly, like a storm sweeping through her mind.

In that moment, she may feel that her present life has been built on a beautiful lie. Sarath's love, his warmth, the laughter of her children—everything may feel strangely distant for a moment.

She will remember Narendran. And the memory of the man she unknowingly left behind may hurt in ways she cannot describe.

But what will she do with that pain?

Narendran recognized her—and yet he walked away. Will she not feel a deep ache knowing that he left without claiming her? She may long to go back to him. But what if Narendran has moved on? What if he has rebuilt his life?

Her other choice is to remain with Sarath—the man who gave her a new beginning, a home, and love. Over the years, she has formed a real bond with him. She may have children who depend on her.

Narendran's sacrifice might haunt her forever—or she may keep her old love tucked away in a quiet corner of her heart, like a cherished but unreachable dream. Her life becomes a blend of old sorrow and new joy, past grief and present affection.

Sarath, too, faces a complicated truth: the woman he loves once belonged to another man.

Love That Remains

In ***Innale***, memory becomes a delicate bridge between what we once were and who we grow to be. Identity shifts, reshapes, and forms new stories when the old ones are lost. A woman rebuilds herself from nothing, letting new affection guide her wounded mind. A man from her past carries a love she cannot recall, held captive by memories she no longer owns.

Two lives drift forward—one freed by forgetting, the other bound by remembrance. The film reveals a gentle psychological truth: identity is fluid, love intertwines with memory, and the heart learns to survive even when the mind rewrites its story.

Life does not always return what it takes away. Lost truths do not always wait to be found. Yet between yesterday and today lies a small kindness—the strength to love again, the courage to release the past, and the quiet hope that what slips away from memory may still bloom deep within the soul… in another time, another place, another tender tomorrow.

Chapter 10

Yakshi

Yakshi is a 1968 Malayalam psychological thriller directed by K. S. Sethumadhavan and written by Thoppil Bhasi, based on Malayattoor Ramakrishnan's novel of the same name. The film stars Sathyan, Sarada, Adoor Bhasi, N. Govindankutty, Bahadur, Ushakumari, Sukumari, Rajakokila, and Radhika. It is widely regarded as the first psychological thriller in Malayalam cinema.

Psycho-Social Analysis

Sreenivasan (Sathyan) is a chemistry lecturer, popular among the girl students at his college. Outside the classroom, his great passion is researching fairies and Yakshis. In the staff room, his colleagues mock this interest. They argue that a man of science believing in such things is shameful. One of them even asks how a scientist can hold on to such myths.

Sreeni replies that although he does not fully believe in them, he cannot claim with certainty that they do not exist. He reminds his colleagues that science still knows very little about many things, and that it is arrogant to accept only what is visible to the naked eye as truth.

Sreenivasan is in love with his colleague Vijayalakshmi (Ushakumari). While continuing his research on fairies, he even goes to meet a sorcerer. His friend warns him that he is becoming obsessed and that the whole thing looks ridiculous from the outside.

Sreeni then shifts into a new bungalow. The house carries a grim story. On the wall hangs the portrait of a woman—a Yakshi, the ghost of a woman who died in a strange and tragic way. She was a gifted dancer, betrayed by her lover. Sreeni tells his girlfriend this sad tale, and both of them feel frightened by it.

Vijayalakshmi warns him that Yakshis crave the blood of young men. She asks whether it is safe for him to live there alone. Sreeni becomes restless and uneasy. The very next day, due to his carelessness, an explosion occurs in the chemistry lab. His once handsome face is horribly disfigured. Devastated, he watches everyone who once adored him now shrink away in fear and disgust.

Within days, he meets a beautiful woman named Ragini (Sarada). In spite of his disfigurement, Ragini accepts him without hesitation. They get married and enjoy a period of happy married life.

However, the peace does not last. Slowly, Sreenivasan begins to suspect that Ragini is a Yakshi. He starts seeing "proof" everywhere. He dreams that she wants to drink his blood and gain immortality.

Conformity Bias

Here we can view his thinking through the lens of 'conformity bias'—the tendency to interpret every new experience in a way that fits what we already believe.

As Sreeni's mental health worsens, no one can pull him out of his fixed belief that Ragini is a Yakshi. Chandran suggests that Sreeni's sexual inadequacy is the real reason behind these ideas. But Sreeni twists this weakness into a kind of "protection" that nature has given him against Ragini. He insists that if he ever gives in to physical intimacy with her, she will kill him.

Next door, Kalyani—who has already reached menopause—suddenly becomes pregnant. Sreeni becomes certain that Ragini will destroy the pregnancy. Ragini, on the other hand, takes care of Kalyani with genuine concern. In his research, Sreeni has read that Yakshis are especially fond of human fetuses. This fits his fear perfectly.

One night, Kalyani miscarries. Ragini is with her when it happens.

Later that night, Sreeni wakes to the sound of chilanka—ankle bells—and a haunting song. Fully awake now, he sees Ragini slipping out of the house. A strange, unearthly glow surrounds the paala tree (milkwood pine) nearby.

Tension between the couple rises. Sreeni finally loses control and tries to kill Ragini. She escapes only because Chandran arrives at the right moment. Chandran and his wife quickly send Ragini back to her parental home. Hoping to save what is left before things get worse, Sreeni's friends tell him the true story of the unlucky girl Ragini.

Sreeni's mind softens. Realizing how much he misses her, he decides to bring her back.

But things fall apart again.

The next day, Ragini is nowhere to be found. Sreeni says that when he rejected her, she vanished into a cloud of smoke, snatched away by a Gandharva who lived in the paala tree. In his rage and despair, he cuts down and destroys the tree.

Is Sreeni's account true? What really happened to Ragini? Was she actually a Yakshi who disappeared in a flash of light and smoke, as he claims? Or has his trauma twisted his mind beyond recognition?

'Yakshi' tells the story of a man who loses everything he loves. Malayattoor Ramakrishnan wrote the original novel in such a way that readers are never sure where logic ends and imagination begins.

After Ragini's disappearance and Sreenivasan's bizarre behaviour, the police take him to a psychiatrist. Sreeni insists Ragini was a Yakshi and that she vanished from his sight. No one believes his story. The psychiatrist explains to the police that Sreenivasan has become mentally ill because of his obsessive thoughts about Yakshis. Eventually, Sreeni confesses that, in a moment of severe mental disturbance, he killed Ragini.

Psychological Dimensions

Identity Collapse

Sreeni's brilliant, handsome face is ruined in the lab accident. In a single night, his identity, self-confidence, and masculine pride crumble. After the incident, students mock him, women avoid him, his friends pull away, and society turns its face from him. This breaks his mind. The film shows how public shaming and rejection can push a person toward mental illness. Here, we see the early seeds of paranoia.

Body Dysmorphia

He becomes obsessed with how he looks, constantly worrying about how others see him. He grows hypersensitive and increasingly isolated. After the accident, no woman looks at him with warmth—only fear or disgust. This is not just a feeling in his mind; he is truly cut off from affection and acceptance.

Fantasy vs. Fear

Then Ragini appears—a beautiful woman who loves him without any conditions. But Sreeni's mind is now fragile. He cannot believe that someone so lovely could love a man as disfigured as he is. Doubt creeps in like a black serpent.

Mental Illness and Myth

As Sreeni's insecurity intensifies, his thoughts twist into dangerous shapes.

He begins to see Ragini's beauty as threatening. Her calmness seems suspicious. Her unconditional love feels unnatural.

Sreenivasan develops symptoms of paranoid personality disorder. We must remember that even before the accident, he was deeply preoccupied with the idea of Yakshis. So when a beautiful woman appears and accepts him despite his scars, he "fits" her into that myth—she must be a Yakshi.

His belief in myths slowly hardens into fixed delusions. These delusions grow into a more serious condition: delusional disorder, and finally paranoid schizophrenia. In the end, he kills his loving, innocent wife and is sent to prison as a man completely lost to madness.

Mental Illness and Society

In the 1960s, awareness about schizophrenia in Kerala was very limited. Before modern treatment became common, people mostly explained unusual behaviour through beliefs in spirits, ghosts, and fairies.

Even speaking about mental illness made many people uncomfortable. That is why, in the film, the concept of Yakshi is used as a cultural frame to talk about a serious psychiatric condition.

Paranoid Personality Disorder vs Paranoid Schizophrenia

Paranoid personality disorder is an anxiety-based condition. In the past, it was considered a mild mental illness or neurosis. People with this problem—often described as suffering from "suspicion disease"—see others through a lens of constant doubt. They believe people are trying to cheat, harm, or humiliate them.

Because they trust no one, everyone around them gradually turns into a potential enemy in their mind. They start to avoid relationships and withdraw socially. Their fear makes them search for "evidence" that supports their suspicions.

Paranoid schizophrenia, however, is a psychotic disorder and much more serious. Their beliefs can become strange and hard to accept. They might think that aliens are following them, or that secret groups such as the Illuminati, or powerful figures like Elon Musk, Bill Gates, or the Chinese government are watching them.

They tell these stories with full conviction because they truly believe them. Hallucinations and delusions are common. Many are sure that organizations, companies, or governments are stealing their thoughts or reading their minds using advanced technology.

In ***Yakshi***, the central character Sreenivasan is shown as someone who ultimately suffers from paranoid schizophrenia and kills his wife Ragini under its influence.

Cinema, Shadows, and a Fractured Mind

Often celebrated as Malayalam cinema's earliest psychological thriller, ***Yakshi*** grows out of Sreeni's unsettling feeling that there might be another world beyond what science can grasp—a secret realm with its own laws, shadows, and cruel magic. In that hidden space, the impossible feels natural, and the film explores how such unseen fears spill into a man's daily life.

Sathyan—fondly remembered as "Satyan maash"—gives one of his finest performances as Sreeni, the rational academic whose mind begins to crack after deep physical and emotional wounds. His breakdown is slow, quiet, and painful. We watch him change from a cheerful, logical teacher into a man trapped in his own nightmares, unable to separate vision from reality. He clings to his fantasies because, for him, they are safer than the truth. With half his face scarred, he carries most of his madness in his eyes—eyes filled with suspicion, hurt, and unbearable loneliness.

Sharada is unforgettable as Ragini. She moves like a puzzle—gentle yet mysterious, never completely ordinary, never entirely supernatural. Is she just a simple woman pulled into Sreeni's life by chance? Or is she the Yakshi he believes she is? Her performance holds the audience between compassion and dread.

Adoor Bhasi, Sukumari, Bahadur, and the rest of the supporting cast bring warmth and weight to the story. Under K. S. Sethumadhavan's assured direction, and through Thoppil Bhasi's script, Malayattoor's disturbing tale comes alive on screen with quiet intensity. The tension builds slowly, tightening step by step as the film moves toward its grim conclusion.

When we compare the film with the novel, the movie offers a more direct explanation for what happens, likely because Sethumadhavan approached the story with a more rational outlook. The book, told through Sreenivasan's fragile viewpoint, refuses to settle on a single truth.

Was Ragini taken away by some otherworldly power, as Sreeni swears? Or did his broken mind create a nightmare he could never escape? Both feel painfully possible, leaving some questions forever hanging between reality and imagination.

The film's ending brings a bit more clarity than the novel, perhaps more than needed—but even so, 'Yakshi' remains one of Malayalam cinema's most memorable psychological dramas. Supported by Devarajan's music and Vayalar's soulful lyrics, the film still feels powerful and haunting, untouched by the passing of time.

Chapter 11

Vidheyan

Vidheyan is a 1994 Malayalam film written and directed by Adoor Gopalakrishnan, adapted from Zakariya's novel 'Bhaskara Patelar and My Life'. With Mammootty and M. R. Gopakumar in the lead roles, the story unfolds in the rustic landscape of South Karnataka. The film received the National Film Award for Best Feature Film in Malayalam, and Mammootty won the National Award for Best Actor for his haunting portrayal of Bhaskara Patelar. It also earned multiple honours at the Kerala State Film Awards.

'Vidheyan' is far more than a tale of a master and his submissive servant. It uncovers deep layers of psychology and power that run beneath the surface of human relationships. Only when we read Zakariya's novel and watch Adoor's film do we fully grasp the rare brilliance of Adoor Gopalakrishnan's direction. The film itself becomes a study text for anyone who wishes to understand cinema. Here, it is impossible to clearly declare who is the hero and who is the villain. The narrative moves through the inner lens of Thommi's mind, portrayed with quiet power by M. R. Gopakumar.

Through this story, Zakariya and Adoor reveal how power can deform a person's soul, how the strong shape the thoughts of others, and how the weak sink slowly under the burden of dominance.

Bhaskara Patelar (Mammootty)

Bhaskara Patelar stands as the very image of cruelty. He does not hesitate to wound, humiliate, or destroy. He demands absolute obedience, and the people around him respond with fear, helpless respect, and silent resignation. Patelar is the raw face of male domination—the dark force of unchecked authority.

Psychopath

Like many psychopathic personalities, Patelar carries deep narcissism and a pleasure in causing pain. He keeps a gun with him always—a clear sign of violence and command. Though he holds no real legal power, he behaves as if he alone rules the land.

He bends any situation to satisfy his wishes. The suffering of others gives him satisfaction, and he uses every tool—money, strength, and sex—to keep his control firm. He stays in power by frightening people and crushing their dignity. At the same time, he knows how to lure and bind others—gifting saris, offering food, drawing women into emotional dependence.

Patelar repeatedly insults Thommi without cause. He kicks him, spits on him, and shames him publicly. When he notices Thommi treating Yusuf with respect, Patelar grows uneasy. Seeing Yusuf as a danger to his absolute rule, he immediately sets out to weaken him and reduce him to nothing.

Beast

Patelar cannot be imagined as a man with conscience. From small wrongs to brutal crimes, he performs everything with chilling ease. In one unforgettable scene, he chases a young girl carrying firewood. He hunts her like a wild animal, with the ferocity of a tiger closing in on its prey. After overpowering her, he turns to Thommi and asks whether he, too, wants to take advantage of her—like a beast offering its prey to another. Adoor frames Patelar beneath a buffalo horn, making his inhuman nature unmistakable. Even the way he eats meat resembles an animal tearing into flesh.

Saroja (Tanvi Azmi)

Saroja, Patelar's wife, is gentle and moral, a woman who tries to guide her husband toward what is right. Patelar sees her goodness as a threat. Slowly, without reason, he becomes convinced that she must be removed from his life. Dictators, and all who are drunk with power, share this weakness—they cannot tolerate questions, doubt, or honesty.

Patelar's insecurity becomes fully visible in the way he treats Thommi. He wants Thommi always beside him—silent, obedient, and fully surrendered. He wants Thommi to remain at his feet forever. As Zakariya writes and Adoor portrays, Patelar is the last shadow of an old feudal world, towering above everyone yet deeply afraid of losing control.

Thommi (M. R. Gopakumar)

Thommi stands as a quiet reminder of how deeply power can shape a human life. A migrant worker who has come to a strange land looking for safety and survival, he carries the struggles of countless people who once travelled to the Malabar region to build a living in harsh conditions. Bhaskara Patelar chooses Thommi as the first target for his cruelty. He humiliates him, beats him, and even violates Thommi's wife, Omana. Though Thommi briefly threatens to kill Patelar, he eventually realizes that he has no strength against this man. Slowly, helplessly, he bends.

This surrender becomes something much darker. Thommi slips into a state similar to Stockholm syndrome. In time, he becomes Patelar's most faithful servant, accepting every blow, every insult, every cruelty. At one point, he tells Patelar that his wife carries the scent of Patelar's perfume. It is not a metaphor. It is the tragic truth of a man who has given up his entire self to the person destroying him.

The End of Patelar

The villagers, long crushed under Patelar's brutality, finally turn against him. They chase him for his violence, his crimes, and for murdering his wife. Patelar runs in fear, and Thommi—still bound to him by invisible chains—tries desperately to protect him. But Patelar cannot escape. Saroja's brothers catch him and kill him.

Adoor frames these moments with remarkable insight. When a wild tiger wanders into a village and harms people, the locals chase it back into the forest, and later, out of fear and anger, they hunt it down. Patelar meets the same fate. A man once praised for his power becomes only a beast to be destroyed. The villagers free themselves by ending the last shadow of feudal rule.

Thommi collapses in grief, crying from afar like a dog mourning the death of its master. In that moment, the animal inside him—the part that lived only to obey—dies as well. But soon, something rises in its place. Thommi picks up Patelar's gun, the symbol of all the power that enslaved him, and hurls it into the river. With that act, he releases himself. He steps out from the darkness of the forest and runs toward the light of the village, a free man for the first time.

In the Workshop

'Vidheyan' remains one of the greatest works of Adoor Gopalakrishnan, Mammootty, and M. R. Gopakumar. Few actors of Mammootty's stature would have dared to play such a terrifyingly negative role. And Gopakumar, through Thommi's wounded silence, delivered a performance worthy of the highest honours.

Learned Helplessness

Dr. Martin Seligman's famous experiment on dogs at the University of Pennsylvania explains Thommi's condition with painful clarity. When dogs were placed in a cage where shocks could not be avoided, they eventually stopped trying to escape. Later, even when they were moved to a cage where a simple lever could stop the shocks, they did nothing. Their earlier suffering had already taught them that escape was pointless.

The same pattern appears in human beings. People who stay in destructive situations—even when a way out exists—often do so because their minds have accepted helplessness as a way of life.

Stanford Prison Experiment

Dr. Philip Zimbardo's 1971 experiment showed how easily human beings misuse power. Students assigned as "guards" began to torture the "prisoners," even though the setup was only a simulation. The uniforms, the authority, and the sense of control awakened hidden cruelty. Power, even when imaginary, can turn ordinary people into oppressors.

Stockholm syndrome

Stockholm syndrome occurs when victims form emotional bonds with their captors. This survival response appears in cases of kidnapping, child abuse, sexual violence, and domestic terror. In the 1973 Stockholm bank robbery, hostages even defended their captors afterward. Thommi's loyalty to Patelar is an echo of this same survival instinct.

Sociological Symbols

In Adoor's hands, Thommi becomes the very image of the oppressed. Though he appears weak, it is through his eyes that the story is told. He is a man stripped of identity, clinging to obedience because he knows no other way to live.

Thommi's submission is a form of psychological bondage—not chains made of iron, but chains built from fear, dependence, and humiliation. Patelar and Thommi together form the perfect outline of oppressor and oppressed.

Every violent act becomes a sign of a larger truth:

- Patelar abusing villagers reflects systemic oppression.
- Patelar humiliating Thommi mirrors rigid class hierarchy.
- Patelar's sexual violence shows the entitlement of patriarchy.
- Patelar killing a dog suggests how power turns cruelty into entertainment.

Violence becomes the language through which Patelar rules and the method by which society maintains order.

Patelar's wife, Saroja, stands as a quiet emblem of women who suffer in silence—women crushed under patriarchy, without escape or support.

And at the heart of it all lies a simple message:

Oppression does not survive because the oppressor is strong.
It survives because the victim is afraid.

Chapter 12

Thanmathra

Thanmathra (2005), written and directed by Blessy, is one of Malayalam cinema's most tender explorations of memory and loss. Starring Mohanlal, Meera Vasudevan, and young Arjun Lal, it is inspired by Padmarajan's short story *Orma*. The film gently follows the life of Rameshan Nair (Mohanlal) as Alzheimer's disease slowly unravels the world he once knew.

The movie received wide acclaim, winning five Kerala State Film Awards—Best Film, Best Actor, Best Director, Best Screenplay, and a Special Mention for Arjun Lal. It also earned the National Award for Best Feature Film in Malayalam at the 53rd National Film Awards.

Rameshan Nair is diagnosed with dementia at an unusually early age. For many Malayalis, *Thanmathra* became their first close encounter with the reality of Alzheimer's. Blessy portrays Rameshan's decline with quiet honesty—his forgetfulness, the slipping of words, the changing of mannerisms, and the slow fading of his once-sharp mind. Mohanlal delivers these moments with heartbreaking simplicity, allowing the audience to feel each small loss as deeply as the character does.

But the film goes further. It shows that the weight of this illness does not fall on the patient alone. Those who care for him—his wife, his children, and his loved ones—carry a heavier burden. Their fear, exhaustion, and helplessness are depicted with the same compassion as Rameshan's struggle.

In countries like the United States, millions are devoted to supporting caregivers of Alzheimer's patients. The therapist in the film explains why this support is crucial: when families collapse under strain, the patient suffers even more. Alzheimer's usually progresses slowly, but when it appears early in life, the decline can be swift, often leading to death within three or four years.

Thanmathra remains one of Malayalam cinema's most moving portraits of how memory shapes identity, and how its loss reshapes every life around it.

Chapter 13

The Bridge

In the 2009 anthology 'Kerala Café', the short film "The Bridge" tells the moving story of an elderly woman living with dementia. As her condition worsens, her family decides they can no longer care for her. One of the most painful moments comes when her son takes her to a movie theatre, hoping the outing will lift her spirits. But halfway through the film, she wanders out and disappears. Along with 'Thanmathra', this segment helped many viewers understand the emotional and physical strain carried by families who look after loved ones with dementia.

Bridge (Eighth Segment)

Bridge is rich with symbols of loss, loneliness, and quiet suffering. The narrative unfolds in two parallel threads. The first follows a young boy and his beloved kitten. In an attempt to discipline the child, his father throws the kitten away. The child, overwhelmed by grief, becomes sick. Filled with remorse, the father searches everywhere for the kitten to comfort his son, but he cannot find it.

The second story follows a young man living in severe poverty. Unable to cope with the demands of caring for his frail, aging mother, he abandons her on the roadside. His desperation hardens into cruelty as he walks away, leaving her alone in the world.

In the final moments, both abandoned beings — the lost kitten and the deserted mother — find each other. They remain together on the verandah of Kerala Cafe, two lonely hearts sharing a small island of warmth in a world that has forgotten them.

Psycho-Social Analysis

'The Bridge' is a gentle yet piercing look at what abandonment does to the human spirit. Through the mirrored stories of a discarded kitten and an unwanted mother, the film reveals the deep wounds created by fear, pressure, helplessness, and emotional collapse.

The Psychology of Abandonment

In both narratives, abandonment arises from distress, not hatred.

- The father throws away the kitten as a misguided punishment.
- The son deserts his mother because poverty and caregiving have drained his strength.

This reflects a pattern known as avoidant coping — when emotional strain becomes unbearable, people sometimes run away instead of facing the struggle. The kitten and the mother stand for all those who suffer because someone else could not bear life's weight.

Learned Helplessness

Both abandoned figures show the quiet, painful acceptance seen in cases of learned helplessness.
The elderly mother, lost in dementia, no longer has the ability to resist.
The tiny kitten, powerless to defend itself, simply endures.

Their stillness becomes the film's strongest voice, echoing the silence of countless neglected lives.

The Burden of Caregiving

The young man's decision to leave his mother speaks to a harsh truth: caring for someone with dementia can overwhelm even the most loving families. His act is heartless, yet the story hints that extreme stress, poverty, and loneliness can push a person toward choices they would never imagine making.

Instead of blaming the individual, 'The Bridge' urges viewers to see the larger crisis — families break when society offers no support.

Guilt and the Wounded Child

The father believes he is teaching his son discipline, but instead he wounds the child's heart. The boy's illness shows how emotional hurt can appear in the body. The father's frantic search for the kitten becomes a symbol of regret — a reminder that the fears and feelings of children are often far deeper than adults realize.

Comfort in Abandonment

The final image — the old woman and the kitten resting side by side — carries the soul of the film. Two forsaken beings, joined by their shared sorrow, create a moment of peace for each other. Psychologically, this resembles trauma bonding: those who share the same kind of pain often form the most tender and healing connections.

A Quiet Message to Society

The film gently exposes how poorly society supports the elderly, the poor, and emotionally vulnerable children. When systems fail, families are left alone to carry impossible burdens — and even love begins to crumble under the pressure.

The Bridge holds up a mirror to our lives.

It reminds us that hardship can turn gentle hearts into silent wrongdoers, that fear and exhaustion can erode compassion, and that even good intentions can end in tragedy. Yet the film leaves us with a small, luminous hope: even in the darkest corners of loneliness, a little kindness can still survive.

Chapter 14

Sapthamashree Thaskaraha

Sapthamashree Thaskaraha (Seven Good Thieves), released in 2014, is a Malayalam heist comedy written and directed by Anil Radhakrishnan Menon. The title, drawn from Sanskrit, means "Seven Good Thieves." In the film, one of the central characters undergoes a striking change in personality after suffering a head injury. His reactions slow down, his thoughts seem muddled, and the sharpness he once had begins to fade.

By the final scenes, he is shown sitting with one crore rupees in his hands — a fortune beyond imagination — yet his face shows no excitement or understanding. He stares at the money as though it means nothing to him. That quiet moment carries a powerful truth: a single injury to the brain can reshape a person entirely. It reminds us that who we are — our choices, our emotions, even our sense of value — rests within the fragile structure of the brain, and that trauma can shift everything.

This type of change closely resembles a condition known as frontal lobe syndrome. It refers to a set of neurological problems caused by injury to the prefrontal cortex, the part of the brain that guides our judgment, personality, behavior, and drive. Damage in this region can arise from head trauma, strokes, dementia, or tumors, and it often leads to profound changes in how a person thinks, responds, and understands the world.

Through a single character and a single scene, the film gently shows how the mind can be altered, and how a once-familiar person can become almost unrecognizable after injury.

Chapter 15

Ormayundo Ee Mukham

Nithya, a gifted sand artist, loses her ability to hold on to new memories after an accident. She can only remember a single day at a time. To make sense of her world, she writes down everything in a diary so she can rebuild her life each morning. Gautham, a young businessman who struggles with small memory lapses of his own, grows tired of his mother pushing him toward a marriage he doesn't want. To escape this pressure, he pretends he is already in love and goes out looking for someone who can help him maintain the lie.

During an early morning walk, he meets Nithya. Something about her gentleness draws him in immediately. They spend one beautiful day together, and very quickly, love begins to bloom. But Nithya refuses to write about him in her diary. She believes that if they are truly meant to be, she will remember him on her own.

The next day, she forgets him completely.

With the help of Gautham's friend Apoorva and Nithya's sister Neetu, he keeps visiting her, hoping her heart will find him again. Over time, the warmth between them returns. Gautham finally brings her home and tells his family that she is the woman he loves. But Nithya, weighed down by the reality of her condition, tears out every memory of him from her diary. She tells him that their future together is impossible.

They go their separate ways.

Later, on his way to the United States, Gautham meets Neetu, who shows him a video of Nithya's sand art. To his shock, the shapes and patterns in the sand reflect moments connected to him. He stops his journey and rushes to see her performance. When she spots him in the crowd, her hands move instinctively, and she shapes his face in the sand — even though she claims she cannot recall who he is.

In that quiet moment, they both understand the truth: even if her memory fades every day, her love does not. They marry and find happiness together.

Medico-Psychological Analysis

The entire emotional weight of the film rests on Nithya's memory loss. Her condition, described as anterograde amnesia, forms the base of the romance. But while the story is tender and touching, the medical understanding behind her illness is deeply flawed.

Medical Inaccuracies

In the movie, Nithya wakes up each morning with her memory wiped clean, unable to remember anything beyond the day of her accident. The film suggests her brain "resets" every 24 hours, returning her to a fixed point in the past. It calls this anterograde amnesia — a disorder where the brain loses the ability to create new long-term memories.

However, real anterograde amnesia does not behave this way. There is no automatic daily erasing of memory. People with true anterograde amnesia remain forgetful and often confused, but they do not experience complete resets at exact intervals. They also retain their habits, routines, and procedural skills.

In the film, Nithya remembers her sister, her home, her daily surroundings, and her diary — and she remembers to read it every morning. Such selective memory is medically impossible. A person cannot lose an entire day's experiences yet hold on to complex emotional and contextual memories so clearly.

Psychological Truths

Even though the medical portrayal is unrealistic, the film captures emotional realities with honesty. Nithya forgets Gautham each day, yet her sand art reveals that something deeper lingers in her mind. This reflects a known psychological truth: feelings often survive even when memory does not. Her decision to remove Gautham from her diary comes from fear — a fear many people with chronic conditions experience. She worries she will cause him pain, so she distances herself.

For Gautham, the story shows the burden of caring for someone who may never fully remember you. His frustration, his longing, and his determination mirror the emotional strain many caregivers face.

Though its medical details are incorrect, 'Ormayundo Ee Mukham' succeeds in touching the heart. It gently reminds us that love does not always depend on memory. Sometimes, it lives beneath the surface, returning again and again, even through forgetfulness. The human mind may fail — but the heart often finds its own way back.

Chapter 16

Anantaram

Anantaram (1987) stands among Adoor Gopalakrishnan's most puzzling and psychologically layered creations. Written, directed, and produced by Adoor himself—and carried by unforgettable performances from Ashokan, Mammootty, and Shobana—the film unfolds like a quiet confession. Every moment comes to us through the voice of the central character, as though he is speaking from the depths of his own mind, trying to piece together the story of his life. For its time, this approach felt entirely new.

The film received the FIPRESCI Award at the Karlovy Vary International Film Festival and won three National Awards: Best Director, Best Screenplay, and Best Audiography. Years later, in an IBN Live poll, it found a place among the 100 greatest Indian films.

What makes *Anantaram* truly enchanting is Adoor's refusal to explain anything. He gives us no guidance, no clear meaning. Instead, he leaves open spaces, almost like unfinished thoughts, inviting the audience to fill them with their own understanding. Some viewers feel the film uses elements of magical realism, much like Gabriel García Márquez's novels. Others believe Adoor was portraying a deep psychological struggle. Adoor himself says nothing—allowing multiple truths to coexist.

One of the most discussed readings of the film is this: Ajayan, the young narrator, is abandoned as a baby. A compassionate doctor takes him in and raises him with affection and discipline. But Ajayan never escapes the quiet ache of being unwanted. After the doctor's death, he clings to his foster brother Balu for emotional support. Everything changes when Balu marries Suma (Shobana). Ajayan becomes painfully drawn to her, ashamed of his feelings, and eventually runs away.

From here, the film begins to drift into the uncertain territory of a mind under strain. Ajayan meets a woman named Nalini, who feels strangely familiar—almost like Suma appearing in another form. Whether Nalini is real or a creation of Ajayan's longing is never made clear. As the narrative splits, Ajayan gives two different versions of his life. Each contradicts the other. His inner world seems to divide into separate voices, each claiming to be the truth.

Some believe these contradictions hint at schizophrenia—Ajayan's identity fraying under emotional stress. Others insist it is magical realism—life seen through the eyes of a deeply wounded child who grew into a man terrified of belonging. Whatever interpretation one chooses, Ajayan's struggle is deeply moving. He searches for clarity but keeps drifting further from himself.

This leads to the question that has followed the film for decades:
What was Adoor really trying to say?

Only Adoor knows. And he chooses to stay silent.

That silence may be the film's greatest gift. *Anantaram* does not offer explanations. Instead, it holds up a mirror—still, unsettling, and endlessly open to interpretation. It reminds us that the mind is not a simple, orderly place. It is a tangle of old wounds, scattered memories, unspoken desires, and fragile dreams. Some memories guide us; others deceive us. Some voices comfort; others confuse.

In the end, 'Anantaram' is not merely the story of what happens to a young man. It is the story of a mind bending under its own sorrow. It shows how identity, longing, and loneliness can entwine until the borders between truth and imagination blur.

And perhaps that is Adoor's quiet message:

Some mysteries are not meant to be solved. They are meant to be felt—left open, like Ajayan's story, which never truly finds an ending.

Chapter 17

Njangalude Veettile Athidhikal

Njangalude Veettile Athidhikal (2014), directed by Sibi Malayil and written by K. Gireesh Kumar, brings Jayaram, Priyamani, Narain, and a strong supporting cast into a story that moves gently between sorrow and psychological unraveling. With Bijibal's haunting music beneath it, the film slowly shifts from a family drama into a quiet reflection on how grief can break the human mind when it arrives without warning.

The Shattered Home

Advocate Manoj Kumar and his wife Bhavana live a simple life in the city with their young daughter. Manoj spends his days chasing cases, clients, and status. Bhavana, more withdrawn, finds comfort only in her books. Though their worlds seldom meet, they continue alongside one another—until a sudden accident takes their child away. From that moment, their home, once alive with laughter, becomes a space filled with silence, sorrow, and unspoken wounds.

Unable to face his pain, Manoj hides behind work and forced outings. Bhavana, trapped in her own loneliness, begins to drift into a deeper emotional void. Her grief becomes a doorway through which fear and confusion slowly enter.

Onset of Breakdown

As time passes, Bhavana's thoughts grow tangled. Ordinary conversations feel threatening. Simple phone calls seem suspicious. Her sorrow takes the shape of a dangerous belief—Manoj is being unfaithful. Instead of turning to him, she confides in Maya, a well-meaning friend who unintentionally leads her further off course. Maya suggests a reckless idea: if she feels betrayed, she should create an affair of her own.

In Bhavana's fragile state, the thought takes hold. She begins writing letters to one of Manoj's clients, a criminal. But in her imagination, his face changes—she replaces him with the handsome model she sees each day on a billboard. Soon, this imagined man steps into her home, speaks to her, and comforts her. To Bhavana, these visions feel as real as any living person.

Facing the Invisible Enemy

Manoj eventually finds her speaking to empty space. At first, it terrifies him. Slowly, he understands—something inside his wife is slipping away. He meets a psychiatrist, and Bhavana is diagnosed with a psychotic disorder. The doctor advises him to patiently help her question the false stories created by her mind.

Manoj reshapes his life around her healing. He follows her fragile moods, persuades his parents to do the same, and gently introduces small doubts into her imagined world. Over time, the presence of her fantasy lover fades.

But the story takes an unexpected turn: the real criminal receives her letters. Touched by her words, he reforms and comes searching for her. In that moment, imagination and reality stand side by side, blurring the lines in Bhavana's mind even further.

Narrative Weaknesses

Despite heartfelt performances, the film makes several medical missteps:

- Bhavana's delusions are labeled "schizophrenia," though psychosis has many forms.
- Most people with such illnesses show negative symptoms—emotional flatness, slow thinking, withdrawal—which the film ignores.
- It suggests that love alone can cure mental illness, a common cinematic myth. In truth, proper treatment requires medication, therapy, and long-term psychiatric support.

These are familiar errors in Indian films, where complex brain disorders are often reduced to dramatic visions and simple emotional resolutions.

The Psychology of Pain and Love

Yet, for all its scientific flaws, *Njangalude Veettile Athidhikal* beautifully captures how grief can bend a person's reality. Bhavana's decline is not sudden—it is a slow drowning, hidden behind quiet days and unreadable silences. Manoj's struggle mirrors hers; loving someone who vanishes into an unseen world is its own kind of suffering.

The film gently reminds us that when tragedy enters a home, the true "guests" that follow are fear, guilt, confusion, and unspoken sorrow. And unless they are recognised early, they settle deep into the heart.

In the end, the story is not only about mental illness. It is about a fragile marriage held together by two wounded people trying to keep their world from collapsing. It shows that love can support and guide—but true healing asks for understanding, medical care, and the courage to seek help before the darkness becomes too deep to escape.

Chapter 18

Veruthe Oru Bharya

Veruthe Oru Bharya (A Wife for Nothing), released in 2008, is a Malayalam family drama written by K. Gireesh Kumar and directed by Akku Akbar. Starring Jayaram, Gopika, and Nivetha Thomas, the film became a huge commercial success and struck a deep emotional chord with audiences across Kerala.

Sugunan and Bindu live under the same roof, yet lead completely separate emotional lives. Sugunan, a rigid government employee, believes a wife exists only to serve—cook, clean, press his clothes, and follow his every command. Bindu works endlessly to keep her home running, but her love and labour go unseen. Every day, instead of kindness, she receives criticism. Instead of care, she faces humiliation. At times, his cruelty even crosses into physical hurt.

Over the years, Bindu's spirit slowly withers under the weight of this neglect. Even her family is not spared from Sugunan's harshness. When he publicly insults them, and later shows no emotion at her mother's death, something inside her finally collapses. His angry slap becomes the final wound. She walks away, seeking shelter in her parental home, asking Sugunan to look after their daughter on his own.

Left suddenly alone with his child, Sugunan begins to realise a truth he had never cared to see—parenting demands patience, warmth, and emotional presence. But when their daughter narrowly escapes an assault during an outing, terror grips him. The guilt of failing her twists something deep inside his mind.

Persecutory Delusions

This shock triggers a dangerous change in Sugunan's thinking. Ordinary sights and sounds begin to feel threatening. He becomes certain that invisible enemies are waiting to harm his daughter.

He disconnects phone lines, drives visitors away, and views even familiar faces with suspicion. This is more than anxiety—it is persecutory delusion, a severe mental state in which the mind invents threats and believes them as absolute truth.

These delusions isolate him completely.

They turn affection into danger, silence into fear, and every shadow into a possible attacker.

In one tragic moment, overcome by terror rather than anger, Sugunan harms his daughter while trying to "protect" her from an imagined threat. This heartbreaking mistake forces everyone around him to confront the reality of his unraveling mind.

Beyond the Marital Frame

When Bindu returns to support the family after this crisis, the film reveals its deeper psychological message:

Unseen emotional wounds can grow into walls inside the mind.
Unhealed shock and guilt can twist themselves into paranoia.
Fear, when left alone too long, becomes a monster larger than any real-world danger.

Persecutory delusions do not appear in a single day—they rise slowly from stress, loneliness, shame, and the unbearable weight of responsibility. Once rooted, they distort a person's world so completely that even love becomes unfamiliar.

Closing Argument

'Veruthe Oru Bharya' becomes much more than a portrait of a troubled marriage. It turns into a quiet, but powerful reminder of how emotional neglect can destroy a woman's inner life, and how untreated fear can push a man into a frightening mental breakdown.

The film teaches us that families do not break only through arguments—they also collapse through silence, indifference, and the refusal to understand one another. And true healing begins not with blame, but with empathy, awareness, and the courage to reach out for help before the mind sinks into darkness.

Chapter 19

Vadakkunokkiyanthram

Vadakkunokkiyanthram (Compass), released in 1989, is a Malayalam black comedy written and directed by Sreenivasan, who also plays the lead role alongside Parvathy. The film examines how a marriage slowly unravels under the weight of Othello syndrome — an intense, irrational form of jealousy. It received three Kerala State Film Awards, including Best Film, and was later dubbed or remade in several languages: Telugu (*Sandeham*), Tamil (*Dindigul Sarathy*), Kannada (*Nanjangudu Nanjunda*), and Hindi (*Main, Meri Patni Aur Woh*).
Even today, this film remains one of Malayalam cinema's most memorable works, cherished for Sreenivasan's rare blend of humour and insight.

Although remembered for its comedy, the film hides a deeper, painful truth beneath the laughter. It follows Thalathil Dineshan, a soft-spoken printing press owner whose sense of self has been shaped — and scarred — by the world around him. His short height and dark complexion are pointed out to him repeatedly, until he quietly accepts that he is somehow "less" than other men.

When he marries Shobha, a woman who is graceful, educated, and taller than him, his already fragile confidence begins to crumble. In a society that teaches men to feel superior to their wives, Dineshan sees her beauty not as a blessing, but as a threat. From this seed of insecurity begins a downward psychological spiral.

His worries slowly grow into Othello syndrome, a rare condition where jealousy turns into delusion. Ordinary actions begin to look suspicious. Reassurance sounds like hidden deceit. His mind locks itself behind a door where reason cannot enter.

From a sociological view, Dineshan is the result of a culture that ties masculinity to height, fairness, dominance, and control. He feels he must constantly prove his worth. This pressure pushes him into comical — and tragic — attempts to appear more "manly," to imitate others, to force confidence he does not feel. His own brother's charm becomes a danger. A passing look from a stranger becomes a threat. His marriage becomes a stage for battles that exist only in his imagination.

Shobha, gentle and loyal, becomes the silent casualty of his illness and the society that shaped it. Nothing she does can quiet the fears that have taken over his mind. In time, his delusions grow so intense that those around him fear for his wellbeing. He is admitted to a psychiatric hospital.

For a while, treatment brings peace. But the film ends with a scene that chills the heart. While Shobha sleeps, relieved that life feels normal again, Dineshan wanders outside, searching the night for enemies that exist only in his thoughts.

This closing moment reveals the film's deepest truth: insecurity, once fed by social expectations and left untreated, can follow a person like a shadow for life.

'Vadakkunokkiyanthram' is far more than a comedy. It is a sharp psychological and social reflection — a tale of how fear distorts the mind, how patriarchy fuels doubt, and how love suffocates when trust is replaced by suspicion.

Chapter 20

Ulladakkam

Kamal's **Ulladakkam** is far more than a psychological thriller. It is a tender, unsettling look into how trauma reshapes a life, how memory twists under pain, and how society misunderstands what it cannot see. Adapted by P. Balachandran from Cherian Kalpakavadi's story and brought to life by Mohanlal, Shobhana, and Amala Akkineni, the film remains one of Malayalam cinema's most emotionally layered works. It earned several Kerala State Film Awards—Best Director, Best Actor, Best Dubbing Artist—and won Amala a Filmfare Award for her unforgettable performance.

The film begins with a dream: Dr. Sunny (Mohanlal) wakes in terror after finding himself lost inside a vast mental maze. This dream quietly becomes the film's central symbol. In 'Ulladakkam', the mind is portrayed as a world with many doors—some beautiful, some locked, and some hiding shadows no one wishes to face.

Though Dr. Sunny appears calm and steady, the case he takes on soon tests the very limits of empathy. Reshma (Amala), the younger sister of his best friend, is found trembling in a ruined room, frozen with fear and unable to grasp reality. At the hospital, she sits in silence, her eyes vacant, as if her spirit has stepped away from her body. Her diary reveals early emotional wounds—losing her mother as a child, and an earlier brief psychotic break. But Sunny slowly uncovers the deeper fracture in her mind: Reshma watched her lover Arun being murdered on the beach, powerless as the sea swallowed him. That trauma had settled deep in her unconscious, returning now as nightmares, dissociation, and a crippling fear of the ocean.

Through hypnosis and gentle exposure therapy, Sunny helps her confront the memories she buried. The terror begins to fade, but another emotion rises in its place. Her long-starved need for love and safety attaches itself to Sunny. In her vulnerable mind, he becomes a substitute for Arun—a classic case of transference. She clings to him, mistakes kindness for affection, and wraps her entire healing around his presence.

Sunny recognises the danger, but the world around them does not. As someone remarks, psychology may explain Reshma's behaviour, but society refuses to understand it. When she overhears that Sunny does not return her feelings, she retreats into silence once more. To everyone else, it seems the crisis has ended. But deep inside her mind, the unresolved wound of Arun's death continues to throb.

At Sunny's wedding, the sound of drums—Arun's instrument—shatters her fragile balance. In a violent surge of psychosis, she kills Sunny's wife. Her conscious mind had recovered from fear, but her deeper pain had never been touched. Therapy had eased the trauma, but not the insecurity and emotional dependence that lived beneath it.

Reshma's story reflects the painful truth of those who carry early emotional losses. Their longing for love becomes intense, and their minds often drift into PTSD, dissociation, and breakdowns under unbearable stress. *Ulladakkam* portrays this vulnerability with rare honesty, and Ouseppachan's music deepens every moment, echoing her loneliness and desperation.

Ultimately, the film leaves us with a lingering ache: sometimes the heart survives what the mind cannot.

The Mind's Dark Corridors

Amala's portrayal of Reshma renders her more than a patient—she becomes the living form of trauma. Two profound losses define her life: her mother's death in childhood, and the violent loss of Arun. PTSD takes hold of her, revealing itself through dissociation, trembling panic, and emotional emptiness. Beneath these symptoms rests a deeper wound: the desire for love and stability that life repeatedly denied her.

Blindness to Invisible Suffering

The film shines a quiet light on how society treats trauma. Suffering becomes gossip, not concern. Emotional need becomes scandal, not a plea for safety. Reshma's pain is misread by the world around her, illustrating how easily society condemns what it refuses to understand.

Borrowed Emotions

Sunny enters her life with responsibility and compassion, but Reshma's vulnerable mind turns him into a figure of emotional rescue. Transference blurs her perception, and the weight of this misplaced love falls heavily on Sunny. Their psychological entanglement becomes the heart of the film's tension.

The Sea as the Gatekeeper

The ocean becomes a symbol of her unconscious—vast, frightening, and filled with memories too painful to face. Every wave echoes Arun's death, reminding us that trauma lives in the senses long after logic forgets.

Cinema and Psychological Reality

Although the film presents trauma with genuine emotional depth, it simplifies therapy for dramatic effect. Healing appears faster, hypnosis seems more powerful, and recovery looks cleaner than in reality. Yet these choices do not weaken the emotional truth of the narrative—they simply reflect the needs of storytelling.

The Final Breaking Point

Reshma's healing was only partial. Her dependency and grief were never addressed. When Arun's memory resurfaces through music at Sunny's wedding, the last barrier in her mind collapses. Her violent reaction is not rooted in malice; it is the eruption of pain that was left untouched.

Mirror Held to the Mind

Ulladakkam asks us silent but aching questions:

How much sorrow can a mind endure?
Why do we judge the wounded instead of helping them?
What happens when grief and longing collide inside one fragile heart?

Reshma's journey shows that psychological wounds do not disappear with time or temporary calm. They wait—quietly, patiently—until a sound, a face, or a memory pulls them back to the surface.

The song *Pathira Mazhayeto*, composed by Ouseppachan and sung by Yesudas, remains etched in Malayali memory. Kamal frames it with extraordinary grace. Ashokan's quiet, broken portrayal of Arun stays long after the film ends. And when these performances merge with the haunting presence of Mohanlal, Murali, Amala, and the rest of the cast, 'Ulladakkam' leaves behind a sorrow that lingers—soft, deep, and unforgettable.

Chapter 21

Identity

Identity (2025) is a Malayalam action-thriller crafted by Akhil Paul and Anas Khan, produced by Confident Group and Ragam Movies. With Tovino Thomas, Trisha Krishnan, and Vinay Rai leading the cast, the film began its journey on 25 November 2022. Shooting started in Goa on 12 September 2023, and Jakes Bejoy shaped its music and background score. Released on 2 January 2025, the film drew mixed reviews, but its psychological layers sparked wide discussion.

The Story Begins

Identity opens like a long, dim hallway where each doorway reveals a new face—and every face hides another mind beneath it.

Amar Felix works at a clothing store, but the trial rooms hide the darkness he carries. He films women without their knowledge, blackmails them, and ruins families for profit. His abandoned warehouse becomes the grave of his crimes when a stranger steps in one night, kills him without hesitation, and burns the place to erase every trace.

Weeks pass before the next shadow enters the frame: CI Allen Jacob. Sharp, charming, and carefully unreadable, he approaches DYSP Dineshan with an eyewitness—Alisha, now renamed 'Ann' to protect her identity. She insists she can recall the killer's face. Dineshan places both her and Allen in a safe house.

In that same building lives Haran Shankar, a quiet karate teacher scarred by a violent childhood. His obsessive routines, emotional distance, and rigid habits reveal a young man who has learned to survive by hiding inside himself.

A simple moment exposes Haran's hidden talent—his ability to sketch faces with uncanny detail. Allen immediately recruits him to draw the murderer. But when Ann describes the killer, Haran's own face appears on the paper. Suspicion spreads through the room. Allen takes him to the crime site for another attempt. This time, the face Ann describes belongs to someone entirely different.

But the truth is far more tangled—Haran himself killed Amar.

When Haran realizes Ann's memories could lead to him, he enters her house secretly, only to be caught by his uncle, Dr. Sudarshan. Ann threatens them with a gun, but Sudarshan notices something unusual: she cannot recognize faces at all. Allen comes in, calling her by her true name—Alisha—and the truth unfolds.

Four weeks earlier, Alisha, a news presenter, uncovered Amar's hidden crimes with the help of a hacker. But when she attempted to expose him, she was caught in the fire Haran set. She escaped onto the road, where a truck struck her, leaving her with prosopagnosia—a neurological condition that erases the brain's ability to recognize faces.

Allen tries to arrest Haran. But suddenly Ameer Ali arrives, claiming he killed Amar. Later, Haran reveals the truth—Amar had assaulted his sister Neerja and her friend Sakina. Sakina's brother Ansar came to him in despair. That night, Haran killed Amar. Ameer, wanting to save his son, stepped forward to take the blame.

But behind all this lies a larger predator. Allen disappears from the scene, leaving behind the scent of corruption. Haran realizes Allen is searching for Amar's hard drive, which contains videos of his crimes. A violent chase follows. Allen steals Haran's disguise, fools Dineshan, and murders him for the hard drive. Alisha misunderstands Haran—but soon learns the truth.

Slowly, Allen's true identity emerges. He is a suspended officer who turned the Witness Protection Scheme into a criminal business, selling false identities to dangerous people. Chinappa, a powerful businessman, was one such client. When Chitrammal, a journalist's widow, resisted her forced identity change, she became a target. Allen hired Amar to trap Ansar into helping kill her mid-flight.

But Amar abducted Neerja and Sakina instead, setting off the chain of destruction.

Now Allen holds Devika and Neerja hostage at a hospital. Police question Dr. Sudarshan and discover who Haran really is—a former NSG commando and an active Sky Marshal.

Haran boards the same flight as Chitrammal. With help from Alisha and Nakul, he identifies other witnesses whose identities Allen sold. Allen's final plan is terrifying: he aims to crash the plane by forcing an air traffic controller to obey him. Haran disables the transponder, prevents the disaster, and saves everyone. Allen escapes but loses Amar's hard drive after it is destroyed by MRI radiation.

Weeks later, Allen attempts to escape on a private jet. Fate gives Haran one last chance. Assigned as Sky Marshal on that flight, he confronts Allen high above the clouds. In a fierce mid-air battle, Haran kills Allen and his men, ending the chain of betrayal, manipulation, and death.

The final moments fall into silence. Haran steps out—not as a hunted man, not as a suspect, but as someone who restores stolen identities and protects those who have no one else.

Psycho-Social Analysis

Haran Shankar (Tovino Thomas)

Haran is portrayed as an intense, withdrawn Air Marshal whose mind carries hints of Asperger's syndrome (now part of Autism Spectrum Disorder in DSM-5). People on this spectrum often struggle with social cues, emotional expression, and unspoken meanings. They rely on routines, resist sudden change, and may develop extraordinary skills in specific fields.

Haran fits this profile—emotionally distant, quietly rigid, and obsessively precise. His talent for sketching is remarkable, almost compulsive. His father's strict discipline and his mother's profession as a police sketch artist seem to have shaped both his gift and his emotional boundaries. His world begins and ends in silence, except when he draws. His trauma, especially the violence endured by his sister, fuels his sense of duty and becomes the fire behind his decision to kill Amar.

Alisha (Trisha Krishnan)

Alisha—later called Ann—survives an accident that damages her brain. She loses the ability to recognize faces, even her own. This condition, prosopagnosia, arises when the fusiform gyrus is injured. She sees features—eyes, nose, mouth—but cannot combine them into a meaningful whole. Her descriptions are incomplete, and Haran unintentionally fills the gaps with his own imagination.

Her emotional breakdown reflects the terror of living in a world where every face is a stranger. She can no longer trust memory, instinct, or perception. Her confusion becomes a central thread of the story.

Allen Jacob (Vinay Rai)

Allen begins as a confident Circle Inspector, but the plot slowly reveals his moral decay. He becomes cunning, calculating, and ruthlessly violent. Psychologically, Allen represents an important truth: identity is not fixed. It bends under pressure, changes with circumstances, and sometimes splits entirely. He becomes a man shaped by greed, power, and secrecy—a dark mirror to Haran's inner discipline.

Identity is built on an intricate screenplay that constantly challenges the viewer. Its ideas are brilliant, its psychological themes compelling, but its ambitious complexity sometimes weighs it down. Yet beneath the uneven execution lies a striking exploration of the human mind—fractured, fluid, and always shifting.

The film reminds us that every person carries more than one self. Identity is not a single mask but a shifting reflection, changing with memory, trauma, fear, and the choices we make in silence.

Chapter 22

The Auspicious Omen — The Psychology of Time

The Myth of "Right Time"

People often say, 'His time was wrong,' 'This is the curse of bad timing,' or 'We were born at the wrong hour.' These sentences sound ordinary, almost harmless, yet they reveal something deep about the human mind. In India especially, time is not seen as neutral. It is treated as powerful, even divine. The exact second of birth is believed to decide intelligence, success, marriage, illness, and death. Today, this belief has gone so far that some families schedule cesarean deliveries to match an astrologically "perfect" moment, as if destiny can be edited like a calendar entry.

Behind this belief lies the idea that distant stars—many of which burned out millions of years ago—and planets like Mars, unimaginably far away, are shaping our daily lives. The moon is often given special importance, with claims that it controls emotions and behaviour. In reality, while the moon can move entire oceans, its gravitational effect on a human body is weaker than the pull of a mosquito sitting on your skin. The belief survives not because it is true, but because it is comforting.

Mind Needs Meaning

This is not about mocking superstition. It is about understanding why the mind clings to it. Human beings struggle with uncertainty. Randomness feels cruel. If events are accidental, then suffering has no reason, and success has no guarantee. The idea of "auspicious time" protects us from this discomfort. It gives chaos a story.

But when we look closely at life, time does not behave like a god. It behaves like chance.

Three Scenes, One Truth

Consider three simple scenes.

In the first, a man visits a fortune teller at exactly 10:30:15 a.m. He steps out at 10:32:10. At that precise moment, a vehicle turns the corner at high speed and kills him.

In the second, on another day, he exits at the same time. His phone rings. It is an unwanted call. He hesitates, annoyed, and loses fifteen seconds. He reaches the road at 10:32:25. The same vehicle has already passed. He lives.

In the third, the scene repeats. The phone rings again. This time, he ignores it. He reaches the road at 10:32:25. The vehicle arrives at that exact second and kills him.

Nothing mystical changed. No planet shifted. No star intervened. Only timing—pure, indifferent randomness.

Life Without Design

Every life-altering moment works this way. The friend you met because you were late. The job you lost because you fell sick that morning. The person you married because you chose one seat instead of another. A decision made while hungry is not the same decision made after rest. Anger, weather, health, mood, fatigue—tiny variables quietly push life in different directions.

We like to believe that success follows a formula. That is why books promising 'Seven Steps to Success' sell in millions. They offer control. They suggest that life is a staircase if you just follow the steps. But real life is not a staircase. It is a crowded street full of sudden turns, collisions, delays, and escapes.

Success is not only talent and effort. It is also survival. It is being at the right place when disaster misses you by seconds.

History's Accidents

History itself is built on accidents. Wars, famines, personal losses, and sudden courage shaped the people we now call great. Gandhi did not emerge from comfort. He was shaped by oppression. Without injustice, there would be no Gandhiji as history knows him. If he were born in a different time, in relative comfort, he might have been dismissed as impractical, even irrelevant.

Greatness is not planned. It is forged in unpredictable conditions.

The Nature of Time

Time is not divine, and it does not sit in judgment over our lives, rewarding some while punishing others. It does not plan, prepare, or arrange outcomes with intention or mercy. Time simply moves, indifferent to hope and fear alike. It is unpredictable, shifting without warning, careless of our beliefs about fairness or destiny. And in the quiet space between seconds—between a phone ringing and staying silent, between one step taken and one delayed—entire lives are altered forever, not by design, but by chance.

Chapter 23

Akashadoothu

Akashadoothu is a 1993 Malayalam family drama directed by Sibi Malayil and written by Dennis Joseph, starring Madhavi and Murali in powerful lead roles. The story follows the heart-shattering journey of a mother diagnosed with leukemia, inspired by the 1983 American film 'Who Will Love My Children?'

The film received overwhelming critical acclaim and became a massive box-office hit, eventually becoming the highest-grossing Malayalam film of its time. It ran in theatres for more than 365 days and is considered one of the most influential melodramas of the 1990s. It won the National Film Award for Best Film on Family Welfare, and Madhavi earned the Kerala State Film Award for Second Best Actress as well as the Filmfare Award for Best Actress.

Over the years, 'Akashadoothu' has gained cult status and is widely regarded as one of the finest emotional dramas in Malayalam cinema. Its impact led to remakes in Telugu ('Matrudevobhava'), Kannada ('Karulina Koogu'), and Hindi ('Tulsi').

When Bond Becomes Home

Johnny (Murali) and Annie (Madhavi) grow up together in an orphanage. What begins as childhood companionship grows into deep love, and later, a marriage filled with hope. Their modest home is lit by the laughter of four children:

- **Meenu**, the eldest, already motherly

- **Rony and Tony**, eight-year-old twins, inseparable
- **Monu**, the baby who fills the home with sunshine

Johnny earns a living driving a jeep, while Annie teaches violin, filling the neighbourhood with soft music. They live simply, but with love—except for Johnny's occasional drinking, which brings shame and sadness into the home.

Cruelty and Unseen Tragedy

One morning, a proud milkman, Keshavan, argues with Johnny and walks away humiliated. Later, seeing Tony cycling alone, he hits the child with his van out of anger. Tony survives, but the hospital reveals Annie's devastating secret—late-stage leukemia. Her time is short.

Johnny breaks down, quits drinking instantly, and stays close to his family. For a brief time, life softens.

Fate Strikes Again

As Johnny rushes home with Annie's medicines, he encounters Keshavan again; another fight ends in a tragic accident. Johnny is gone forever.

Annie stands alone—with death approaching and four children who depend on her completely.

A Mother's Greatest Fear

Annie and Johnny were orphans. Her deepest fear is not dying, but leaving her children to the same fate. Quietly and with immense courage, she begins searching for loving families who can raise them.

To protect her children, she lies gently:

"I must go to Germany for work. New parents will care for you until I return."

Meenu, wise beyond her age, already knows the truth. She and Annie hold each other, promising silence and strength.

Finding New Homes

With Father Vattappara's help:

- **Monu** is adopted first by a loving doctor and his wife
- **Tony** finds a home after hesitation from many families due to Rony's disability
- **Meenu** begs to stay, but Annie whispers, "Shine brightly… so I can find you everywhere."

Only **Rony** remains.

One Last Christmas

Annie's strength is fading, but she dreams of one last Christmas together—filled with cake, lights, and love. She writes a letter to Meenu: *"Never lose your brothers. Keep our circle unbroken."*

The Stillness of the Heart

On Christmas Eve, she dreams of her children running to her. She wakes with a soft smile, but the room is empty. A thin line of blood slips from her nose. Kneeling before the crucifix, she whispers:

'Just one more day… just one more hug.'

A deep stillness fills her. Later that night, Rony wheels himself into her room and finds her lying peacefully, with a faint smile still on her face.

The Farewell

At the funeral, the children stand with their new families, trying to grasp the enormity of their loss. When the moment comes to part, heartbreak fills the air.

As Father Vattappara prepares to take Rony back to the orphanage, a car returns. Tony leaps out before it stops and runs to his brother. His adoptive father steps forward and says:

'There's room for one more. Bring Rony too.'

Under the pale winter sun, the twins embrace—together again. Somewhere beyond, Annie's heart surely glows brighter than the Christmas star.

Psycho-Social Analysis of Akashadoothu

The Unique Emotional Impact

Some films are revisited many times— 'Chithram, Vandanam, Chandralekha, Oru Vadakkan Veeragatha, Manichitrathazhu', and many others.
But 'Akashadoothu' belongs to a rare group: a massive hit that people cannot bear to watch twice. Even director Sibi Malayil and writer Dennis Joseph later admitted they themselves could not rewatch it.

The Struggles Behind the Screen

Initial Fear and Rejection

Producers hesitated when they heard the script. They feared:

- the cast might not attract crowds
- the sorrowful subject would fail at the box office
- the film would not recover its cost

The team originally hoped to shoot in Vagamon to create a European setting for "Aaradhike...," but the budget forced them into the rubber plantations of Kottayam. Yet from this limitation emerged magic.

Music That Became Immortal

Ouseppachan and ONV created songs that became part of Malayalam cultural memory. Annie's violin and the haunting melodies stirred deep emotion.

A Song That Became Legend

The entire orchestra recorded live at Sujatha Theatre while watching the film projected on the big screen. The conductor, who didn't understand Malayalam, broke into tears from the emotional weight. The female singers repeatedly stepped out to compose themselves. Musicians cried while playing.

Even today, Yesudas' voice in that song instantly brings Annie's fragile, loving face before the viewer.

From Failure to Phenomenon

Despite its brilliance, the film opened poorly. Small theatres, empty seats, quick removals. Sibi Malayil and Dennis Joseph pleaded with producers for more publicity. No one believed in the film anymore.

Dennis even sent his assistant daily to buy and tear up twenty-five tickets—just to keep the show running.

Producer Kariyachan wept, convinced everything was lost.

The Moment Everything Changed

One evening, as Dennis bought his usual 25 tickets, two college excursion buses arrived. The neighbouring theatre was full. Dennis hurried to the teachers and urged them to try 'Akashadoothu'. They agreed.

The students walked in laughing. They walked out silent—faces wet with tears.

Word spread overnight. Crowds arrived in waves. Families carried towels, knowing the film demanded tears.

Kariyachan announced a prize: A Maruti 800 car to anyone who could watch the film without crying.

From the edge of failure, the film soared into the hearts of a generation.

Akashadoothu won:

- National Film Award for Best Film on Family Welfare
- Kerala State Award (Second Best Actress) for Madhavi
- Best Singer (K.J. Yesudas)
- Best Child Artist (Seena Antony)

A film that almost vanished became one of the most beloved and painful cinematic experiences ever made.

More than a film 'Akashadoothu' is a testament to:

- a mother's courage
- a child's longing

- the devastating weight of separation
- the miracles that shape cinema

And above all, it reminds us that sometimes a single, unexpected moment can lift a story from despair to immortality.

Chapter 24

Njan Gandharvan

Njan Gandharvan—which means "I am Gandharva"—is a 1991 Malayalam romantic fantasy written and directed by the incomparable P. Padmarajan. Nitish Bharadwaj and Suparna Anand bring the story to life in the lead roles.

The film offers a dreamlike tale: a lonely young woman stumbles upon an old wooden idol washed ashore. From this carving emerges a radiant Gandharva—visible only to her. What begins with curiosity soon deepens into a love that is both enchanting and forbidden.

When the film released, audiences were startled. The tender, beautifully filmed intimate scenes upset many, and the movie failed at the box office. Only years later did it gather a quiet, devoted audience who admired its haunting atmosphere, daring narrative, and ethereal beauty.

Trouble had surrounded the making of the film, and just weeks after its release, Padmarajan passed away unexpectedly. These tragedies fed a whispering superstition—the so-called "Gandharva curse"—the belief that any story about a Gandharva invites misfortune upon those who tell it.

Plot

The Statue on the Shore

During a college excursion to the beach, Bhama, a calm and thoughtful final-year student, notices a small wooden figure half-hidden in the sand. The softness of its expression draws her in, and she quietly slips it into her bag.

That evening, alone in her hotel room, she sets the carving on her pillow. A shimmer of light fills the space, a warm breeze brushes her face, and suddenly a striking young man leans over her and places a tender kiss on her lips before vanishing like mist. Bhama sits frozen, heart racing, unsure if she is awake or dreaming.

A Voice in the Breeze

Back home, the presence returns. While studying, she senses someone near her. She steps into the garden and sees a bright blue butterfly circling a tree. A gentle voice whispers, "I am a Gandharva... and I have already fallen for you." When Bhama shyly asks him to appear, he materialises before her—tall, warm, and graceful. "Call me Devan," he says. Bhama feels her heart give way completely.

A Grandmother's Tale

Confused yet mesmerised, Bhama asks her grandmother about Gandharvas. The old woman's eyes light up as she describes celestial musicians born from Brahma's breath—wanderers who play divine music. When they break heavenly commandments, they are banished to earth, living in pala trees, meeting mortal girls, loving them with impossible devotion, then disappearing forever.

Bhama turns to Devan with fear. "Will you one day leave me too?"
He holds her hands. "When I return to the heavens, all memory of earth fades from me. But Bhama, I will not go back. I choose you."

He slips a tiny diamond—Rudhiraksham—from his finger. "Kiss this. Wherever I am, I will come to you."

Love That Feels Like a Dream

Pradeep, the young man her parents approve of, tries to win her affection, but her heart is already elsewhere. Devan even visits her home, playing a single tune on his flute. In moments, her mother and grandmother are moved to tears and say, "Marry this boy, Bhama. He feels like he belongs with us."

A Sudden Silence

Then one day, Devan's voice falls quiet. A pala branch breaks and crashes to the ground, its red sap running like blood. A terrible voice from above declares that Devan has broken sacred laws. The king of Gandharvas is coming to seize him.

The lovers try to flee, hands clasped tightly, but the wind stands like a wall before them. Invisible forces pull Devan upward. He touches his lips and shakes his head—Bhama must never summon him with the diamond again.

A Heart Waiting in Pain

Weeks pass. Bhama grows pale, hollow with longing. Her parents finally surrender: "If marrying your Devan will bring back your joy, we agree." When they ask to meet his family, Bhama feels the weight of her secret. She kisses the Rudhiraksham once more. Devan does not appear. Instead, she feels every stroke of punishment falling upon him in the distant heavens. Her tears spill until morning.

The Punished Lover

Seven nights later, Devan returns, bruised and trembling. "They whipped me for singing to your mother and grandmother in daylight," he says softly. "We crossed too many boundaries."

Suddenly a golden cuff burns into his wrist. He tears it away. A mighty voice—Brahma's—fills the night. Devan's worst crime has been uncovered: he wants to remain mortal, to stay with Bhama.

Punishments await him—rivers of fire, iron embraces, floors filled with serpents. The diamond in Bhama's hand turns to pale dust.

A Terrible Choice

Brahma shows mercy in only one way: If Devan takes Bhama's innocence before the seventeenth wind of the night, they will forget each other entirely, and his punishment will soften.
If he refuses, he will become a monstrous being, wandering for a billion years.

Devan looks at her with heartbreak. "I will never hurt you to save myself."

But Bhama places her hands on his face. "If you suffer, I will feel it too. Let me give you this gift. Let me love you fully—even if we wake tomorrow knowing nothing."

Their tears mingle as she draws him into her arms.

That night, under a sky glowing with stars, they share a love so gentle it feels like prayer. When the seventeenth wind arrives, it lifts Devan away like a whisper.

Bhama stands alone, arms wrapped around the fading warmth, crying soft, steady tears that silver the moonlit air.

Somewhere high above, a Gandharva carries the echo of a mortal girl's love—a memory even the heavens cannot erase.

Psycho–Social Analysis

When 'Njan Gandharvan' first entered theatres, it faltered. Audiences objected to the intimate scenes, though they were filmed with grace and sensitivity. Over the years, however, the film rose in stature, becoming a cult classic admired for its visuals, music, and unusual narrative.

The belief in a "Gandharva curse" also grew in the shadows. Some viewers connected the film's troubled production and Padmarajan's sudden death to the superstition that creating stories about Gandharvas invites misfortune.

We often assume that brilliance will be recognised naturally—that good films will succeed because they deserve to. But life rarely follows such hopeful logic. Many worthy films vanish unappreciated. Njan Gandharvan stands among the clearest examples.

Padmarajan was one of Malayalam cinema's most gifted storytellers, deeply committed to artistic filmmaking. He created this film at the height of his creative strength.

Nitish Bharadwaj, beloved as Lord Krishna from the 'Mahabharata' television series, played Devan with a gentle sincerity that fit the role perfectly. This was a time when mythological themes were warmly embraced, long before today's strict expectations about representation and long before the arrival of endless TV channels.

Suparna carried with her the lingering grace of her role in Bharathan's 'Vaishali', where Malayalis had adored her.

The film had everything—Padmarajan's brilliance, a moving screenplay, poetic dialogue, and unforgettable music. Kaithapram's soulful lyrics became even more magical under Johnson Master's compositions, and K.J. Yesudas elevated every song with his divine voice. As one actor said of "Devi Aatma Raagameykan":

"If Dasettan calls out 'Devi' in that heavenly voice... which Apsara would ignore such a call?"

Yet despite these perfect elements, the film collapsed commercially. Even today, those who love 'Njan Gandharvan'—its songs, its characters, its timeless mood—struggle to understand why the audience rejected it.

The hardest truth is this:

Padmarajan left the world carrying the pain of 'Njan Gandharvan's' failure.

A wound he never deserved.

Chapter 25

Puzhu

Puzhu (2022), directed by Ratheena P.T. and written by Harshad, Sharfu, and Suhas, is a psychologically layered drama that examines how caste prejudice, childhood trauma, and authoritarian identity gradually eat away at the human mind. The title, meaning "worm," becomes an overarching metaphor for decay that begins internally long before it appears on the surface. Starring Mammootty as Kuttan, a retired upper-caste former police officer, the narrative unfolds within the suffocating walls of an urban apartment complex that mirrors his own mental claustrophobia. Far from a conventional thriller, 'Puzhu' dissects how deeply entrenched social structures infiltrate personal psychology, ultimately leading to paranoia, isolation, and intergenerational damage. Much like the worm that burrows unnoticed until it consumes its host, the film suggests that prejudice grows silently until it destroys everything it touches.

Plot

The film follows Kuttan, a widower who raises his young son Kichu with unyielding discipline. Their lives run on rigid schedules, exacting routines, and a constant air of control. When Kuttan's estranged sister Bharati returns to the city with her husband Kuttappan, a lower-caste theatre artist, the cracks in Kuttan's carefully constructed world widen. His caste superiority becomes agitated by her inter-caste marriage, and what begins as discomfort soon evolves into obsessive surveillance, overwhelming suspicion, and a fear that the sins he committed in his police career—framing innocent Dalits—are circling back for revenge.

Running parallel to the plot is a theatrical reenactment of the Mahabharata episode of King Parikshit and the serpent Takshaka. In the epic, Parikshit insults a sage, earning a curse that he will be killed by Takshaka within seven days. Despite the king's desperate attempts to escape fate—fortifying his palace, calling the best physicians, and consulting the wisest men—Takshaka infiltrates his defenses disguised as a worm inside a fruit. When the fruit is delivered to the king, the worm emerges, grows into its true form, and kills Parikshit exactly as foretold. The tale becomes a haunting allegory in the film: sin attracts its own punishment, and no fortress is strong enough to keep out the consequences of past violence. Kuttan watches the play repeatedly, unaware that his own life is following the same tragic arc.

Symbolism and Conceptual Framework

Psychological Metaphor

The image of the worm captures the essence of Kuttan's psychological condition. It represents self-inflicted decay, moral corruption, and the gnawing of guilt beneath a polished exterior. The worm remains invisible but active, feeding on the host until collapse becomes inevitable. In clinical terms, it reflects the internality of paranoia—an erosion that begins quietly until it overtakes the mind completely.

Paranoia as Central Theme

Kuttan's paranoia does not appear suddenly. It forms gradually from rigid thinking, hypervigilance, and deep-seated insecurity. Ordinary events become sinister. Innocent gestures feel threatening. His grip on reality loosens as suspicion replaces reason. This trajectory mirrors the clinical evolution from personality-based suspiciousness to full-blown paranoid delusions.

The Authoritarian Personality

Identity Constructed Through Control

Kuttan's identity is built on authority—caste privilege, police power, and a belief that dominance brings order. His childhood in a violent home taught him that fear is the only language people understand. As an adult, he projects this lesson onto his son, his neighbors, and even strangers. His worldview becomes inflexible: obedience equals safety, and deviation equals danger. Such rigidity is the hallmark of an authoritarian personality.

Paranoid Personality Structure

Psychologically, Kuttan displays persistent mistrust, misinterprets harmless actions as purposeful insults, and believes unseen forces are conspiring against him. As pressure mounts, his perceptions harden into certainties, and his isolation deepens. The deterioration of his mental structure occurs silently but relentlessly.

Early Exposure to Violence

Kuttan's emotional life is shaped by a father who ruled through intimidation. Trauma research shows that children who internalize a violent parent's authority often replicate those dynamics in adulthood. Kuttan becomes both victim and perpetrator, carrying forward the same harshness he once feared.

Repetition of Trauma

His son, Kichu, becomes the next inheritor of this cycle. The boy moves through their home quietly, absorbing his father's anger, dread, and commands. Trust is replaced by fear, and affection becomes transactional. The film demonstrates how trauma travels across generations when left unexamined.

Caste as a Psychosocial Determinant

Caste shapes Kuttan's worldview as profoundly as trauma does. His sense of superiority rests on an inherited hierarchy that dehumanizes those outside his "group." His body language, silence, rituals of purity, and language of contamination all reflect the psychological imprint of caste ideology.

The Sister's Marriage as Identity Threat

Bharati's marriage destabilizes him because it dismantles the narrative of caste purity that structures his identity. Her autonomy becomes an assault on his authority. The conflict between them is not merely familial; it symbolizes the friction between oppressive cultural values and individual freedom.

Disruptive Mirror

Bharati embodies emotional independence. Her gentle defiance unsettles Kuttan because she exposes his fragility. Every calm response she offers becomes a mirror to the violence he carries inside.

Emotional Counterpoint

Kuttappan's warmth, creativity, and grounded presence highlight everything Kuttan lacks. Where Kuttan demands obedience, Kuttappan offers compassion. Where Kuttan fears contamination, Kuttappan embraces connection. This contrast intensifies Kuttan's internal rupture.

Escalation of Paranoia

Anonymous notes, imagined threats, and ordinary household noises become evidence of danger in Kuttan's mind. His past police abuses haunt him as karmic retribution, echoing the Parikshit–Takshaka parable. He becomes convinced that someone—perhaps many—is plotting against him, mirroring Takshaka's disguised approach through ordinary means.

Social Isolation as a Contributing Factor

Kuttan withdraws from meaningful relationships. Without corrective feedback, his thoughts spiral unchecked. The apartment becomes a prison, and his mind becomes the jailer.

The Child as Psychological Victim

Kichu's silent rebellion is one of the most heartbreaking elements of the film. He hides snacks from lower-caste homes, lies about friendships, and retreats into fear. The home that should protect him becomes a source of psychological injury.

Emotional Consequences

His emotional world is marked by anxiety and helplessness. The absence of warmth stunts his sense of self, highlighting how authoritarian parenting fractures a child's emotional development.

Psychological Insights

Kuttan's caste bias aligns with social identity theory, reinforcing in-group superiority and out-group hostility. His guilt creates cognitive dissonance, pushing him deeper into denial and paranoia. His obsessive cleaning rituals and preoccupation with purity resemble maladaptive coping mechanisms rooted in fear. The film does not reduce casteism to a clinical disorder; rather, it exposes how cultural conditioning fosters psychological fragility that later manifests as paranoia, detachment, and emotional collapse.

Social Commentary

'Puzhu' challenges Kerala's progressive self-image by presenting an upper-caste protagonist whose inner world is poisoned by the very privileges society normalizes. It critiques police violence, Islamophobia, and caste prejudice without didactic dialogue. Instead, the discomfort itself becomes the lesson. The inclusion of the Parikshit–Takshaka story acts as a moral parable, emphasizing that no amount of power can protect a person from their own moral decay.

Strengths, Flaws, and Impact

Mammootty's nuanced performance elevates the film, portraying Kuttan as both monstrous and pathetic. Ratheena's direction and Theni Eswar's shadow-rich cinematography reinforce the sense of unease, while Jakes Bejoy's music underscores the film's quiet dread. Though the screenplay occasionally feels overloaded with themes and concludes somewhat abruptly, the film remains a powerful exploration of how systemic prejudice becomes personal madness.

In 'Puzhu', the personal and political merge seamlessly. Kuttan's psychological breakdown is not random; it is the consequence of caste arrogance, unhealed childhood wounds, toxic masculinity, and unchecked power. Like King Parikshit awaiting Takshaka's strike, he cannot escape the worm he carries within. The film stands as both a psychological case study and a social indictment, reminding us that prejudice is not merely a belief—it is a slow death that begins in the mind long before it reaches the world outside.

Chapter 26

Guiding Lights of Malayalam Cinema

J. C. Daniel

The life of J. C. Daniel, remembered today as the father of Malayalam cinema, reads like a tragic and moving film—shaped by chance, driven by passion, wounded by rejection, and honoured only after silence had claimed him. His story carries the weight of devotion, humiliation, struggle, and a recognition that arrived far too late.

Daniel was born on November 28, 1900, in Agastheeswaram, Travancore, now part of Kanyakumari. He studied at University College in Thiruvananthapuram, and even as a teenager, his mind was restless and searching. By the age of fifteen, he had already written an English book on Kalaripayattu. The discipline, movement, and drama of the martial art shaped his understanding of performance and planted the seed of cinema in his mind.

The Filmmaking Ordeal

Daniel's love for movement and storytelling slowly turned into a fascination with cinema. He travelled to Madras, hoping to learn filmmaking, but every studio turned him away. Doors closed one after another. He faced contempt, rejection, and mockery. Yet, he refused to give up. Instead of returning defeated, he moved to Bombay, the centre of Indian cinema.

There, Daniel chose a path born of desperation and intelligence. Knowing the truth would block him again, he introduced himself as a teacher from Kerala who wished to learn cinema to educate others. The lie worked. Studios opened their doors. Daniel watched, learned, observed, and absorbed everything. He returned to Kerala with equipment, knowledge, and an unshakable dream.

Vigathakumaran: The Birth of Malayalam Cinema

In 1926, Daniel sold his land for four lakh rupees and founded Travancore National Pictures—the first film studio in Kerala. From this sacrifice was born 'Vigathakumaran (The Lost Child)'. Daniel did everything himself: writing, directing, producing, acting, cinematography, and editing. It was not just a film; it was his life on celluloid.

The film premiered on November 7, 1928, at Capitol Theatre in Thiruvananthapuram. Audiences welcomed it warmly. But society did not. The fury erupted when P. K. Rosy, a Dalit woman, appeared as the heroine. She was attacked, humiliated, and driven away. Screenings were disrupted by stone-throwing. Shows were cancelled. Theatres were damaged.

Though the film earned some money, it was nowhere near enough. Debt crushed Daniel. He sold his equipment, then his home. The studio shut down. Broken and abandoned, he left Kerala.

Abandonment and Late Recognition

Daniel settled in Palayamkottai in Tamil Nadu and lived the rest of his life as a dentist. When he later applied for assistance under Kerala's pension scheme for artists, his request was rejected repeatedly. The reason given was cruelly ironic—he was told he was "not a Malayali" because he was born in Tamil Nadu.

Only decades later, through the tireless efforts of film journalist Chelangatt Gopalakrishnan, did the Kerala government finally acknowledge the truth. In 1992, the J. C. Daniel Award for Lifetime Achievement was instituted in his name.

Yet the question remains unanswered.
Was Daniel's life a success?
Or does true success refuse to fit into neat measures of money, comfort, or recognition?

Udaya Studio

In the fragile early years of Malayalam cinema, one name stood like a pillar—Udaya Studio. When the industry could barely stand, Udaya taught it how to walk. Founded in 1947 by Kunchacko and K. V. Koshy, the studio became the birthplace of films that shaped generations, including 'Vellinakshatram (1949), Bhargavi Nilayam (1950), and Kathasangamam (1965)'.

Financial failure haunted early Malayalam cinema. 'Vigathakumaran' left Daniel bankrupt. 'Marthanda Varma' never reached theatres. 'Balan' survived only because of the generosity of T. R. Sundaram of Modern Theatres. ***Nirmala*** collapsed commercially. Production houses disappeared one after another, and exhibitors depended heavily on films from other languages.

After 'Prahlada' (1941), Malayalam cinema nearly came to a halt. Many believed the dream was over.

Then Kunchacko stepped forward.

With limited resources and no formal training, he took a risk that others feared. And it worked. Udaya Studio soon became technically advanced for its time. Since Kerala lacked trained directors, Kunchacko brought experts from other film industries. Over time, he took full creative control himself.

His strength lay not just in filmmaking, but in organization, production, marketing, and management. Even today, business students could learn from his methods. At a time when films were only black and white, he experimented boldly with colour in song sequences.

Collapse in Transition

By the 1970s, Udaya Studio began to fade. Technology changed. Audiences changed. Cinema itself transformed. In 1987, the studio closed its doors forever. What was once a centre of imagination and labour could not survive the new world forming around it.

Today, Kunchacko's name is spoken less often than it should be. Yet the foundation he laid still carries the industry forward.

Time has a strange habit of celebrating the present with noise and applause, while quietly allowing the pioneers who made that present possible to fade into silence, remembered only by those who pause long enough to look back.

Chapter 27

Shock Therapy and Films

When people hear the words 'shock treatment', fear rises almost instantly. This fear is not limited to the general public; it exists even among educated individuals and medical students. The strongest source of this fear is cinema. Films have repeatedly painted shock therapy as something cruel and terrifying. The most famous example is 'One Flew Over the Cuckoo's Nest', on which 'Thalavattam' was based. Malayalam films like 'Athiran', 'Bhadratha', and 'Patham Nilayile Theevandi' have also reinforced this disturbing image.

But is shock treatment—electroconvulsive therapy, or ECT—really as horrifying as films suggest?

Cinema often shows a violent, uncontrollable patient being dragged into a room and "corrected" with shocks. Sometimes, even a harmless patient is tied down and shocked by mistake. After the treatment, the patient is shown as broken, confused, or permanently damaged. Over time, these repeated scenes have carved a single image into the public mind.

When you hear the words 'shock therapy', what do you imagine? A group of people forcing a screaming patient into a room. The patient being tied to a bed. A wooden block pushed into the mouth. A powerful electric current passing through the body. Violent shaking. Foam at the lips. A moment that looks like death. And finally, the patient waking up weak, silent, and without memory.

This image became so powerful that even the mayor of Berkeley, California once believed it. He banned shock therapy completely, declaring it a criminal act punishable by jail and fines. Only later did the courts overturn the law.

Reality, however, is very different.

What began decades ago as a crude and frightening procedure has today become controlled, gentle, and humane. Modern shock therapy is not meant for violent patients. It is primarily used for people suffering from severe depression, especially when all other treatments have failed.

Before the procedure, the patient is given medication to reduce saliva. Then anesthesia is administered, and the patient becomes fully unconscious. Only after this is a carefully measured electrical stimulus given. It produces a brief seizure lasting about forty-five to sixty seconds. The patient feels no pain and remembers nothing.

Is shock therapy necessary?

In some developing countries, outdated and painful methods are still used, and this continues to fuel fear. But modern ECT has an extremely low death rate—around two to ten cases per one hundred thousand treatments. This is nearly ten times lower than the death rate associated with childbirth.

Like all medical treatments, shock therapy does have side effects, particularly short-term memory loss. Yet for many patients trapped in severe, life-threatening depression, ECT becomes a lifeline. It is often the treatment that pulls them back from silence, despair, and the edge of death, and returns them to a functional, meaningful life.

The fear surrounding shock therapy was not born in hospitals. It was born on screens. And like many fears shaped by cinema, it survives not because it is true, but because it is familiar.

Chapter 28

Bharamaram

Bhramaram (translated as *Beetle*) is a 2009 Indian Malayalam-language road thriller written and directed by Blessy. The film stars Mohanlal in the lead role, with strong performances by Bhumika Chawla, Lakshmi Gopalaswamy, Suresh Menon, and Murali Gopy. Released on 25 June 2009, the film stood apart for its intense psychological depth and emotionally driven narrative. It was not only well received by audiences but also became one of the highest-grossing Malayalam films of that year, firmly establishing its place as both a commercial success and a memorable work in contemporary Malayalam cinema.

'The wrong we do to others never truly disappears; it waits patiently for the day it is remembered.'
— Carl Jung

Unni works as a share broker in Coimbatore and lives a comfortable, settled life with his wife Latha and their young daughter Lakshmi, lovingly called Lechu. Their home is warm, familiar, and secure, built on routine and trust. Into this quiet comfort steps an unexpected visitor, a stranger who introduces himself as Jose. Unni, troubled by his own forgetfulness, allows himself to believe Jose's claim that they were classmates in the seventh standard. Jose is clever, persistent, and unsettling, and he slowly settles into their home, staying longer than welcome. His alcoholism, strange behaviour, and subtle control begin to disturb the peace of the household, creating a growing sense of unease that Unni cannot ignore.

Though Unni tries to dismiss his discomfort, doubt takes root. Something about Jose feels wrong, as if the man carries a purpose hidden behind casual words and forced familiarity. Seeking clarity, Unni turns to his trusted friend and former classmate, Dr. Alex Varghese. When Alex carefully thinks back and checks his memory, he confirms what Unni has begun to fear: there was no classmate named Jose. The stranger's presence is not a mistake—it is deliberate.

The truth, when it emerges, is far darker than either man imagined. Jose is not Jose at all, but Sivankutty, a man whose name has long haunted Unni and Alex. As children, Unni and Alex had accidentally committed a murder, and to escape the consequences, they framed Sivankutty for the crime. His life was destroyed. He was imprisoned, separated from his wife Jaya and his daughter Meenakshi, and marked forever by a crime he did not commit. The men now understand that Sivankutty's arrival is not coincidence but revenge, patiently planned and carefully executed.

Sivankutty forces Unni to accompany him back to his village, demanding that he confess the truth to Jaya and Meenakshi. Along the journey, Unni is overwhelmed by fear and guilt and attempts to abandon the plan and return to Coimbatore, but Sivankutty threatens him and makes it clear there is no escape. Alex, burdened by his own share of guilt, joins Unni, knowing that the past they buried as children has finally risen to claim them.

As they travel together, Unni and Alex break under the weight of what they have done. They confess their crime openly to Sivankutty and agree to reveal the truth to his family, ready at last to face the consequences they avoided for so many years. But when they reach Sivankutty's home, they are met not with anger or confrontation, but with silence. Jaya and Meenakshi are already dead.

Only then does Sivankutty reveal the final truth. His plan had been to bring Unni and Alex there to kill them, to repay their cruelty with blood. Yet something changes when they confess, when they finally accept responsibility for what they destroyed. The revenge he carried for years loses its grip. Sivankutty lets them go, choosing not violence, but release.

A Psycho-Social Reading of Bhramaram

> 'The truth will set you free, but first it will make you miserable.'
>
> — James A. Garfield

'Bhramaram', directed by Blessy, unfolds like a quiet storm. On the surface, it is a road thriller. Beneath that surface, it is a deeply human story about guilt that refuses to die, trauma that has no language, and a society that protects the respectable while destroying the powerless. The film does not rush toward suspense; instead, it tightens slowly around the mind, forcing both the characters and the viewer to sit with discomfort.

Guilt and the Fractured Mind

At the psychological centre of the film lie Unni and Alex, two men who committed a grave crime in childhood and survived by erasing it from their conscious lives. As adults, they are successful, settled, and socially respected—a stockbroker and a doctor. Yet their peace is artificial. It is built on denial. When Sivankutty reappears, they initially fail to recognise him, not because memory has failed, but because the mind refuses to open a door that threatens the self it has carefully constructed. The film shows how guilt, when buried, does not disappear. It returns as unease, suspicion, and fear, quietly corroding the sense of safety.

Sivankutty represents the opposite psychological state. Wrongly convicted, imprisoned, and cast out, his life stopped moving forward at the moment of injustice. His strange behaviour—shifting between childlike humour, sudden silence, and quiet menace—reflects a mind shaped by prolonged trauma. What appears as madness is partly a wound and partly a performance. He unsettles Unni and Alex on purpose, forcing them to feel what he has lived with for years. His presence is not just revenge; it is confrontation.

Where the Mind Slips

The road trip becomes more than movement through space. As the jeep leaves the ordered city of Coimbatore and moves toward the fog-covered high ranges, the external world mirrors the inner journey of the characters. Inside the confined space of the vehicle, titles and professions lose meaning. The doctor and the broker are stripped of authority, reduced to frightened men facing a past they avoided. The jeep becomes a psychological pressure chamber where denial collapses and truth slowly takes control.

This forced journey resembles an unchosen therapy, where escape is impossible. The mind, deprived of routine and safety, is compelled to confront what it has hidden. The film uses this journey to show that avoidance may delay pain, but it also deepens it.

Class, Power, and Social Silence

Beyond individual psychology, 'Bhramaram' delivers a sharp social critique. The injustice at the heart of the story is made possible by class privilege. Unni and Alex belong to a world that protects its own. Sivankutty, an illiterate rural jeep driver, has no such shield. The film exposes how justice often bends toward those with education, voice, and status, while the poor become convenient scapegoats.

Sivankutty's punishment does not end with prison. The greater damage comes from social shame. His wife Jaya is crushed by the label of being married to a "criminal," and her death shows how society punishes not just individuals, but entire families. The silence of friends destroys Sivankutty's life; the judgment of society completes the destruction. The film quietly accuses the collective, not just the individuals.

Truth Without Healing

When Unni and Alex finally confess, the moment feels heavy rather than redemptive. The revelation that Jaya and Meenakshi are already dead underlines a painful truth: confession cannot undo damage. Truth can stop further harm, but it cannot restore what was lost. Sivankutty's decision to abandon revenge after hearing the confession is crucial. What he sought was not blood, but acknowledgment. To hear the truth spoken by those who lived freely while he suffered was, in itself, a form of justice.

The title 'Bhramaram', meaning beetle or wanderer, captures Sivankutty's existence perfectly—a restless soul circling a wound that never healed, unable to settle until the truth is faced.

Echoes of the Film

'Bhramaram' ultimately challenges the comforting belief that wrongdoing can be sealed away without consequence. It suggests that while the law may fail, the mind never fully forgets. Peace built on denial is fragile, and freedom gained through injustice carries a psychological cost that must eventually be paid.

The film does not offer easy closure. Instead, it leaves behind a quiet unease and a lasting insight: truth may arrive late, and it may not heal everything, but without it, nothing truly ends.

Chapter 29

Changing Perspective of Movies

A Mind Drawn to Crime Thrillers

Over the past five years, crime thrillers have swept across Indian cinema and literature. Stories of serial killers, violent deaths, and chilling cruelty—events that should horrify us—somehow become thrilling when viewed from the safety of a theatre or a living room. The fear sharpens our senses, the rush of adrenaline rises, and the gentle release that follows leaves us oddly satisfied.

It is the same psychological rhythm that makes ghost stories so enjoyable.

Why does this happen?

Because human beings evolved to stay alert to danger. Our ancient survival depended on noticing threats instantly. That instinct still lives within us today, even though danger now arrives in the form of entertainment.

The Spectacle of Violence

After the release of the movie 'Marco', many viewers asked why the film was allowed to show such intense brutality. Some wondered how it passed censorship at all.

A High Court judge once observed, "Do people who cut strangers into pieces for money—without even hatred—deserve justice?"

For years, Malayalam cinema has celebrated quotation gangs, and audiences often rewarded those films with success. Heroes boast about killing, and we clap. But if someone on screen simply says, “Take him,” we take offense.

We honour violence, but our sense of dignity grows weaker.

This pattern, shared by filmmakers and viewers, is rich material for criminologists to study.

When films repeatedly show murder, exploitation, witchcraft, racism, and child abuse as casual events, a culture slowly becomes numb. Crimes lose their weight.

Such numbness is dangerous.

Decline of Talent

A look at recent blockbusters reveals an unsettling truth. Many popular films today lack:

- strong, thoughtful scripts
- memorable lines
- emotional richness
- meaningful romance or music
- powerful performances

Even the creators sometimes admit they cannot explain why their films succeeded.

Instead, many rely on nostalgia—old dialogues, familiar background scores, repeated jokes, and revived songs. Creativity becomes repetition.

Why is talent fading?

Because lived experiences have shrunk.

Older generations grew up through poverty, strict social norms, political upheavals, and intense personal relationships. Those experiences gave birth to deep, moving stories. But the world has changed more in the last 20 years than in the previous 200.

Earlier filmmakers treated cinema as their entire world. Their sincerity produced masterpieces. Today, that seriousness is rare—even among those who finance the films.

Music as Emotional Core

In earlier decades, songs carried romance, yearning, sorrow, and tenderness. Hollywood expressed love through physical intimacy; Malayalam cinema expressed it through melodies and poetic lyrics.

That is why children today sing songs recorded long before their parents were born.

Political Correctness

Trying to force every scene into a politically acceptable shape drains the life out of a film. Cinema is meant to show every shade of human existence.

Yet warnings appear constantly on screen:

"Smoking is dangerous."
"Driving without a seat belt is punishable."
"Violence against women is a crime."

But when someone is murdered?
No warning.

The censor logic becomes impossible to understand.

The New 'Normal'

In trying to promote gender equality, society accidentally glamorised harmful behaviours—cannabis, alcohol, drugs, profanity—as signs of freedom.

A movement as powerful as feminism gradually slid into a cultural confusion that even Western nations now regret.

Movies proudly present gangsters, drug use, reckless behaviour, and casual relationships as signs of empowerment.

These, we are told, are the "new normal."

A World Lost in Screens

People open their eyes to social media, eat while scrolling, fall asleep with phones in their hands, and hardly look at the world outside their screens. The younger generation criticizes easily but creates very little.

How can meaningful art emerge from minds that never look up?

Many new writers even boast:

"I don't read books. But I will write."

That single sentence explains the depth of the problem

References

Academic Journals

Balasubrahmanya, KR, & Ratnakaran, B. (2015). Psychiatric disorders in Malayalam cinema: A comprehensive review.***Kerala Journal of Psychiatry*,*28***(1), 115-120.

John, CJ (2020). Depictions of mental health topics in Malayalam cinema: Stigma, suicide, and treatment methods.***Indian Journal of Psychiatry*,*62***(1), 50-55.

Ratnakaran, B., & Anil, S. (2015). The unsound trend in Mollywood: ECT and the negative portrayals of mental illness.***Kerala Journal of Psychiatry*,*28***(2), 200-205.

Thomas, V. (2021). The cinematic construction of schizophrenia and ASD in contemporary regional cinema: A case study of***Athiran***(2019).***Journal of Disability Studies*,*15***(3), 45-60

Scholarly Books and Critical Essays

- Ganguly, S. (2015).***The Films of Adoor Gopalakrishnan: Master and Slave: Vidheyan and the debasement of power***Cambridge University Press.

- Menon, P. (2023).***Liminal resistances: Local subjects in Kerala cinema and literature***.

- Nair, R. (2018).***The psychological gaze: Trauma, identity, and the unreliable narrator in Malayalam film***.

- Zacharias, P. (1992).***Bhaskara Patelararum Ente Jeevithavum***.

- Karthikeyan, R. (2021). From ***Veruthe Oru Bharya***this ***The Great Indian Kitchen***: Female identity in the domestic space.***Feminism in India***.

- Muralidharan, S. (2017). The psychotic gaze: The supernatural and the psychiatric in ***Manichitrathazhu***(1993).***Journal of South Asian Cinema,10***(2), 88-100.

- 7. Menon KV, Ranjith G. Malayalam cinema and mental health. Int Rev Psychiatry 2009; 21:218–23.

- Ratnakaran B, Anil SS, Thomas S, Ampanattu SD. Depictions of mental health topics in Malayalam cinema. Kerala Journal of Psychiatry 2015; 28(2):204-11.

- Baxendale S. Memories Arena't made of this: amnesia at the movies. BMJ 2004; 329:1480–3.

- Balasubrahmanya KR. Njangalude Veettile Athidhikal (2014). Kerala Journal of Psychiatry 2015; 28:115–7.

- Hyler SE, Schanzer B. Using commercially available films to teach about borderline personality disorder. Bull Menninger Clin 1997; 61:458–68.

- Byrne P. Screening madness [cited 2015 Nov 13]. Available from: https://www.time-to-change.org.uk/sites/default/files/film-report-screening-madness-time-to-change.pdf.

- Balasubrahmanya KR. Nee-Na. Kerala Journal of Psychiatry 2015; 28(2):216-8.

- Sartorius N, Gaebel W, Cleveland HR, Stuart H, Akiyama T, Arboleda-Florez J, et al. WPA guidance on how to combat stigmatization of psychiatry and psychiatrists. World Psychiatry 2010; 9:131–44.

- Byrne P. Why psychiatrists should watch films (or What has cinema ever done for psychiatry?). Adv Psychiatr Treat 2009; 15:286–96.

- Cape G. Movies as a vehicle to teach addiction medicine. Int Rev Psychiatry 2009; 21:213–7.

- Fritz GK, Poe RO. The role of a cinema seminar in psychiatric education. Am J Psychiatry 1979; 136:207–10.

- www.kjponline.com
- The Artificial Key to Success Dr Robin K Mathew Writers Pocket 2024
- Jeevitha Vijayathinte Krithirma Thaakkol - DC Books 2025
- Bordwell, David. “Narration in the Fiction Film”, New York, Routledge, 2014, pp 49-50.
- Bakhtin, Mikhail. “Problems of Dostoevsky’s Poetics”, Minneapolis, University of Minnesota, 8th printing, 1999, p 6& p 220.
- Bordwell, David. “Narration in the Fiction Film”, New York, Routledge, 2014, p 212.
- Gopalakrishnan, Adoor. “Director’s Statement”, 2017.
- Raghavendra, M.K. “Philosophical Issues in Indian Cinema: Approximate Terms and Concepts”, New Delhi, Routledge India; 1st edition, 2020, p 121.

Credit for information from the film industry

Safari TV - History Through Me, Amrita TV - Samagamam, Manorama Nere Chuvve, Samakalika Malayalam, New Indian Express

Mr. Dennis Joseph

Mr. John Paul

Sri Babu Shaheer

Shri Vineeth

Mr. Fazil

Mr. Kamal

Mr. Johnson Master

Mr. Ouseppachan

Mr. Ismail Hassan

Sri Siddique - Director

YouTube channels

Film Talks - Sri DeAva Krishnan

Mukesh Speaking -SriMukesh

Lights Camera Action-Shri Shanthi Vila Dinesh

Sanalkumar Padmanabhan-Facebook

This list never ends.

ABOUT THE AUTHOR

Dr. Robin K. Mathew

Dr. Robin K. Mathew is a highly accomplished behavioral psychologist and ethnographer whose expertise is underpinned by extensive, global professional experience and cross-cultural engagement. His career reflects a deep appreciation for the complex socio-economic, ethnic, and linguistic variances shaping human experience, gained through direct interaction with individuals from nearly **90 different nationalities**.

Dr. Mathew possesses a diverse and distinguished professional history, holding roles such as **Research Assistant, Research Associate, Researcher, and Adjunct Faculty** in prestigious international organizations. His multidisciplinary background includes formal education and experience in **Information Technology, Human Resource Management, Psychology, Cyber Forensics, and Cyber Psychology**.

He has contributed his expertise across various esteemed institutions, including the **University of Toronto, University of Michigan, the Indian Institute of Management (IIM), ICFAI Business School, Best Buy, the Royal Bank of Canada, and Thomson Reuters**. These roles have cultivated an unparalleled ability to synthesize insights across disciplines, significantly enriching his psychological analyses.

Over the past twelve years, Dr. Mathew has authored and published **24 books** that delve deeply into facets of psychology and the human condition. Furthermore, he has contributed nearly **600 articles** across a wide range of subjects, published in prestigious magazines both domestically and internationally. His prolific output captures the intricate nuances of human nature, informed by the vast knowledge accumulated throughout his professional journey.

Dr. Mathew is a **Social Psychology Scientist** currently working independently as an analyst for an international media agency.

Other books by the Author:

Malayalam

1. Madamballiyille Manorogikal
2. Chekuthante Panipura
3. Chanakyante Kamukimar
4. Digital Nagavallimar
5. Cyber Parakaya Pravesham
6. Oru Kanyakayude Suvishesham
7. Jeevitha Vijyathinte Krithrima Thakkol
8. Kaanan Desham Thedi Poyavar
9. Geethanjali Voice
10. Raktham Viyarkkunna Kaikal
11. Oru Manashasthraknjanum Sancharikkatha Vazhikaliloode
12. Swargathinteyum Naragathinteyum Thelivukal
13. Bheethiyude Rakshasukal

English

1. Lovers of Chanakya
2. In Quest of the Promised Land
3. I am Akira
4. The Expedition of Nun
5. The Artificial Key to Success
6. The Psychology of Mind Deception
7. Human Algorithm-Cyber Psychology for the Digital Age
8. The Grand Palace of Lucifer
9. The Saga of Nylari
10. The Proof of Heaven&Hell
11. Vampire to The Lady of Fatima

Email: robinkmathew@gmail.com